PRAISE FOR RANDA

Education and Empowerment: The Essential Writings of W.E.B. Du Bois

This is an invaluable contribution to Du Bois scholarship that will appeal to education, sociology, history, and African American studies scholars. Carefully selected, chronologically ordered, and insightfully introduced, Randall Westbrook's *Education and Empowerment: The Essential Educational Writings of W.E.B. Du Bois* deftly demonstrates the wide range and reach of Du Bois' thought—educational or otherwise. Here, Du Bois the proto-critical pedagogist is placed into deep dialogue with Du Bois the proto-critical race theorist, and Du Bois the sociologist is placed into deep dialogue with Du Bois the political activist. Ultimately, an arguably more education-centered and pedagogy-centered but, yet and still, interdisciplinary and intersectional Du Bois emerges from his writings featured in this innovative volume.

—Reiland Rabaka
author of Du Bois' Dialectics, Africana Critical Theory,
and Against Epistemic Apartheid

Randall Westbrook has captured the voice of Du Bois! He has distilled the years of growth and change that Du Bois experienced internally, and projected externally to us, through Grandpa's own words. By doing so with a concise hand, he has made Du Bois much more accessible to modern students and more human to all of us who have known him our entire lives. He has captured the young boy, the intellectual, the agitator and the profound poetic voice in one place. He has made Du Bois come alive once more…

—Arthur McFarlane II
Great-Grandson of W.E.B. Du Bois

Randall Westbrook has made a singular contribution to the study of W.E.B. Du Bois by revealing through his writings a vital aspect of the complicated leader—his lifelong commitment to education. Westbrook makes a compelling case that the foundation of Du Bois' work came from his educational thought. The organization of the book into three sections, beginning with an adolescent Du Bois, shows us the development of his pedagogy. This comprehensive volume is integral to any study of Du Bois, providing a new lens through which to view the formidable leader.

Amy Helene Kirschke
author of Art in Crisis: W. E. B. Du Bois and the Struggle
for African American Identity and Memory

EDUCATION AND EMPOWERMENT

Photograph of W.E.B. Du Bois, 1907. (Courtesy of the
Department of Special Collections and University Archives,
W.E.B. Du Bois Library, University of Massachusetts Amherst.)

EDUCATION

AND EMPOWERMENT

The Essential Writings of W.E.B. Du Bois

W.E.B. Du Bois

Edited and Introduction by
Randall Westbrook

HANSEN PUBLISHING GROUP

Education and Empowerment: The Essential Writings of W.E.B. Du Bois

Copyright © 2014 by Randall Westbrook

21 20 19 18 17 16 15 14   1 2 3 4 5 6

ISBN: 978-1-60182-046-4 (PAPER)

Cover: Photograph of W.E.B. Du Bois, 1907. Used by permission of the Department of Special Collections and University Archives, W.E.B. Du Bois Library, University of Massachusetts Amherst.

Cover and book design by Jon Hansen

Hansen Publishing Group, LLC
302 Ryders Lane
East Brunswick, NJ 08816

http://hansenpublishing.com

TABLE OF CONTENTS

Section III: Able to Lead the World, *Reconsidering the Role of Black Education*, 1914-1948

FOREWORD

How does one truly grasp the essential W.E.B. Du Bois, given the magnitude of eight decades of activism and accomplishment? Is he best understood as the father of America's civil rights movement? the organizer of the Pan-African Congress? or the founding editor of *The Crisis*? Was he a political and social activist, sociologist, intellectual, artist, environmentalist, economist, or ethicist? Dr. Du Bois was all of these and so much more.

And yet, when you peel away the layers, as Randall Westbrook has done in this unique and thoughtful compilation, it is Dr. Du Bois the teacher who resides at the core. From his early writings as a newspaper correspondent in Great Barrington, education was Du Bois' guiding light and primary motivator, his own salvation and the salvation of his people. In his view, literacy was the foundation of an equitable society for all.

Dr. Westbrook's choice to view Dr. Du Bois through the lens of education goes to the heart of who he was, how he thought, and how his work shaped the political and social landscape of African American people. The genius of Westbrook's *Education and Empowerment* is that we see Dr. Du Bois' brilliance in a way that makes this towering individual accessible. On a personal note, it brings new relevance to the work of the W.E.B. Du Bois National Historic Site in Great Barrington and others around the world seeking to preserve the legacy of this hero and intellectual.

Rachel Fletcher
W.E.B. Du Bois National Historic Site
Co-Director, Upper Housatonic Valley African American Heritage Trail

Acknowledgments

Education and Empowerment* is the result of decades of admiration of W.E.B. Du Bois that turned into an edited volume of his work. As he communicated in writing for public consumption for eighty years, it is nearly impossible to fully capture *all* that he tried to convey on any subject. Du Bois is more than worth the effort. Nearing the sesquicentennial of his birth, he stands as a veritable patron saint for African American intellectuals for more than a century. These collected works provide ample evidence of the richness and breadth of Du Bois' role as an educator—collecting them for public consumption was a labor of love.

I could not have considered such a task without the support of a host of persons. There will most assuredly be names missed; for those, my gratitude, while not specifically stated is nonetheless felt.

To Jon, Jody, Abby and Joyce at Hansen Publishing, thank you for your attention, and the many, many hours of work involved in helping me to achieve my dream of sharing my love and knowledge of W.E.B. Du Bois as a true titan in education.

To Rachel Fletcher, Dr. Amy Kirschke, and Dr. Reiland Rabka, thank you for your words of encouragement and guidance as I sought to adequately reflect this underexplored aspect of the Du Boisian intellectual legacy.

To Arthur McFarlane, thank you for your generosity of time and perspective, and for sharing memories of your Great Grandfather.

To my colleagues at Fairleigh Dickinson University Sammartino

School of Education, thank you for providing a supportive and highly charged academic environment. To my former colleagues at Rutgers University, Africana Studies department, with special recognition of the guidance of my mentor Dr. Leonard Bethel, thank you for the encouragement and inspired nudging toward this mark.

To my parents, Stephen and Pearline Westbrook, and to my sister Rovina Westbrook, thank you for support and guiding love; to the memory of my grandparents, Robert and Willie Moore, thank you for wisdom of the ancients.

To my children Aaron and Leslie, lives spent selflessly, innocently inspring my success, you are an enduring sense of pride and joy.

Finally, to my wife Oma, a constant source of inspiration, encouragement, love and patient understanding, my eternal love and gratitude.

EDUCATION AND EMPOWERMENT

Accessing The Bonus Video Content

You can access the bonus video content on YouTube™ by scanning the QR codes in the Video Sidebars. You will need a QR reader application on a smartphone or tablet with wi-fi capability to view them. You may also access the bonus video content via the YouTube™ app or website using playlist "Education and Empowerment by Randall Westbrook" or with this shortened URL: http://goo.gl/LENJKp. You may also access the video content with the individual URL addresses provided under each video description. Data rates may apply depending on your device's data plan and your type of access.

Video Sidebar

Randall Westbrook talks about his inspiration for the title of his book that analyzes the works of W.E.B. Du Bois.

http://youtu.be/AAenJU1lA9o

Video Sidebar

Westbrook describes the three sections of his book that parallel the adult life of W.E.B Du Bois and highlights his works that are most relevant to education.

http://youtu.be/TLM0Hw0tOFU

Video Sidebar

A brief overview of who Du Bois is and his historical significance.

http://youtu.be/A5LQINKn1H4

Introduction–Biographical Perspectives

In a career that spanned eight decades, W.E.B. Du Bois was one of the most influential intellectuals of the twentieth century. His pioneering scholarly work, insightful intellectual analysis, and soaring, unyielding rhetoric played a key role in many of the significant political and social movements for African Americans, from the 1880s to the height of the modern civil rights movement. More than a century after the publication of his seminal works, "The Talented Tenth" and *The Souls of Black Folk*, his words continue to provide a powerful vocabulary for those who seek to articulate self-determination.

Yet for all his acclaim, for all that has been analyzed, and for all that has been written about his life and work, his contribution to educational thought has gone largely unnoticed. Du Bois represented the major progressive counterbalance to the words, work, and policies of educator Booker T. Washington in the final decades of the nineteenth and first decades of the twentieth centuries. He spent much of his working life as a college professor or a university based researcher. Much of his work from 1883 until his death eighty years later revolved around educational themes.

Du Bois was born on February 23, 1868 in western Massachusetts. He attended public schools in Great Barrington (one of the few students of African American descent to do so), and was the sole Negro graduate from the high school during his years there. Du Bois attended Fisk University in Tennessee, where on the strength of his secondary school training, he was placed into the sophomore class. Following graduation from Fisk in 1888, Du Bois enrolled in Harvard University. Two years later, he earned his long-coveted baccalaureate degree from Harvard, continuing on for a Master's degree in history, which he completed in 1891. While considering opportunities for a Ph.D., he successfully applied for a fellowship, which he used to pursue studies at the University of Berlin. An unsuccessful appeal for renewal of funding before the final year of residency was the lone impediment to his earning a doctorate in economics. Returning to the United States, Du Bois completed his doctorate—the first African American to do so—at Harvard University. The sum of all his educational experiences left Du Bois as one of, if not the most credentialed men—Black or White—in the United States at that time.

In 1897, shortly after completing his Ph.D., Du Bois served as principal investigator on *The Philadelphia Negro*, one of earliest sociological studies conducted in the United States, and the first to specifically explore African American life. Later that year, Du Bois was invited to become a member of the American Negro Academy (ANA), a "learned society of Negroes." The ANA presented the first serious threat to Booker T. Washington about the content and purpose of education for African Americans. Shortly after completing *The Philadelphia Negro*, Du Bois led *The Atlanta*

Video Sidebar

Du Bois advocated all forms of education where Washington suggested choosing vocational or intellectual education.

http://youtu.be/CNzK1uFvfM0

University Studies, a longitudinal examination of Black life from 1897 until 1917.

It is important to note that the battles Du Bois fought, first with Booker T. Washington and later as a member of the executive board of the NAACP, were political, but the landscape upon which they were fought was education. However, these conflicts that began as early as the late 1880s, as Du Bois sought to make a name for himself as a scholar-provocateur, and Washington—from the president's chair of Tuskegee Institute (now University) was beginning to make a name for himself as a political leader. The ferocity of these political battles obscure both the eloquence of their debate, as well as the incontrovertible fact that they were fundamentally educators.

In 1903, Du Bois published two of his most famous works, "The Talented Tenth" and *The Souls of Black Folk*. Continuing to confront questions related to "The Negro Problem," Du Bois extended his political influence during this period with work in the Niagara Movement, a political association he and other like-minded individuals developed in 1906 to address issues of importance for Negro advancement. In 1909 Du Bois was a founding member of the National Association for the Advancement of Colored People (NAACP) where he served as Director of Research and the editor of the organization's periodical, *The Crisis*, from its inception in 1909 until 1934, and again from 1944–1948.

In the 1920s, Du Bois was a major force in encouraging African American political engagement through education as well as through the arts. His efforts were central to the period known as the Harlem Renaissance. Du Bois also encouraged African American student activism, which led for the first time to the appointment of African American presidents at several historically black colleges and universities notably, Howard and Fisk Universities. During this period, Du Bois' views were considered

3

by some to be increasingly radical. This perception, coupled with the seeming increasingly conservative policies of the NAACP, left him nearly untouchable as a political force, and ultimately led to his marginalization and departure from the organization in 1948.

In the 1950s, after a series of legal encounters with the federal government, ranging from difficulties that restricted his ability to travel outside the country, to his indictment as a foreign agent, Du Bois was a broken, if somewhat forgotten man on the landscape of African American political thought. Finally granted the ability to travel internationally in 1958 Du Bois left the United States for good in 1961. He expatriated to Ghana where he was accorded many of the honors as an elder statesman that eluded him in the United States. He continued to write and conduct research on the Black experience, including the beginning stages of an encyclopedia on African American life until days before his death, the night before the historic March on Washington on August 27, 1963.

This volume of collected works contains Du Bois' writings that span sixty-five years, beginning with his first writings in 1883 as a fifteen-year-old correspondent for regional newspapers, and ending with a revisiting of his epochal essay "The Talented Tenth." Of the twenty-eight pieces included in this volume, seven were personal correspondences—letters and diary entries. Collectively, these works show a steel-eyed focus on education that has only occasionally been suggested in Du Bois' work.

Video Sidebar

Westbrook talks about the Harlem Renaissance and how Du Bois acted as an advocate for the arts as editor of *Crisis* and *Opportunity* magazines.

http://youtu.be/r35Z59Tzh1w

The first section includes nine newspaper columns written by an adolescent Du Bois between April of 1883 and May of 1885. They represent the first glimpses of the public mind of W.E.B. Du Bois. Although the primary focus was education, these writings show a range of interests and thought, and a level of intellectual maturity that belied his youth. It is interesting to note here that none of the articles contained a bi-line; the only identifying notation at the bottom of most of the articles were the initials "webd." Given this, It is unlikely that readers outside of the immediate western Massachusetts community could have known that the correspondent chronicling events in Great Barrington was a high school student.

Also included in this section is a letter to his mother, detailing a trip to visit for the first time, his paternal grandfather. This letter is revealing in several respects, first in describing his trip, talks about adding his "illustrious name" to a guest book in the Hartford train depot. Glancing backward, such a statement could easily be read as coming from a precocious, however, Du Bois was already well in the midst of writing for public consumption. He had to be aware of the impact of his work, even if only expressed privately and impishly to his "Mam." Throughout this period, during which time also included the death of his mother, he expressed concern about literacy and political relevance in the African American community. This concern was a recurring theme for Du Bois during this period that persisted throughout his career.

The second section begins with Du Bois seeking a fellowship for European study, corresponding with the fellowship chairman, former U.S. President Rutherford B. Hayes. The exchanges go from polite to testy, as the two men not only negotiated eligibility for the fellowship, but navigate the murky waters of racial antipathy—the unspoken knowledge that Du Bois, an African American scholar, if successful during that European sojourn, could return as the most educated man in America. Du Bois realizes this, and in a journal entry, the implications of his impending accomplishments weigh heavily on his mind in "A Program for the Celebration of My 25th Birthday," which is included in this section.

The few years on either side of the turn of the century were productive ones for Du Bois. After European funding is cut short, he returns without the Ph.D., but with no less passion for his life's purpose. He completes the doctorate at Harvard and returns to Tennessee to reflect on his work as a school master a decade earlier. If his disappointment about the perceived impact of the accomodationist words of Booker T. Washington is suggested in "A Negro Schoolmaster in the South," he is clear in his growing displeasure in "Of Mr. Booker T. Washington and Others." Later Du Bois finds himself in Philadelphia with a lead role in ground-breaking research and positioning himself for race leadership. Du Bois' breakthrough year of 1903 included publication of the anthology, *The Souls of Black Folk*; "The Talented Tenth," and the "Training of the Negro for Social Power," two essays which provided a blueprint for education and political empowerment. His esteem for the intellect and race pride shown by Alexander Crummell, who Du Bois considered a mentor and a role model for progressive black leadership. Although he would continue to write for another six decades, it was here that Du Bois first truly began to exhibit and wield his considerable influence as an educational and political thinker.

Prior to his work in the founding of the NAACP, Du Bois helped found "The Niagara Movement." Du Bois' declaration of principles is a blueprint for the type of leadership Du Bois would espouse throughout the 1920s and 1930s. It was during the 1920s that Du Bois sought what he called a "renewed focus" on education. In fact, from the turn of the century, Du Bois never moved too far away from confronting issues of education; he continued his half century affiliation with Atlanta University and wrote regularly about issues of education in *The Crisis* and other venues. In "A Ruling Passion," Du Bois memorialized Joseph Charles Price, the founding president of the historically Black Livingstone College in North Carolina. Du Bois praised Price's molding of Livingstone into "a kind of Black Harvard" and offered Price's blackness (both pigment and ethnicity) as a template for leadership in historically black colleges. His editorial proved to be a sign of things to come, as he led an all-out assault in favor of African American leadership at his alma mater Fisk in the speech "Diuturni Silenti."

Du Bois' prescient political insight appeared to be at its peak when he confronted the issue of school segregation, some twenty years before the Supreme Court's *Brown v. Board of Education* decision, when he declared that the fight to desegregate schools was futile unless it remedied political realities that perpetuated inferior schools and not simply focus on the act of allowing black children to attend school with white children. Later, his backward glance at his concept of the "Talented Tenth" forecast dire consequences for African Americans unless those in a position to lead the race stepped forward to do so. Contemporaneously, the final two works were often viewed as the rantings of an embittered, erstwhile race leader. Glancing backwards, we can see that for all the resistance, Du Bois' vision was as precise as his rhetoric was sharp.

What makes any consideration of Du Bois especially interesting is that his work has been misunderstood and misinterpreted—of-

---

Video Sidebar

Du Bois valued quality education above integrated schools.

http://youtu.be/XHnKLW6Ut70

---

ten by people who are conflicted as to whether they should embrace his thought or dismiss it. They see the enormity of his contribution to Black thought, while literally ignoring the fact that much of his work occurred in an educational context.

The lack of critical analysis of Du Bois' work through a lens of educational thought could be traced to his political prowess. As a "race leader" (a post-Reconstruction term for African Americans who held informal positions of power within the black community), the core of his authority was as political as it was informal. Where these conflicts took place or the combatants—whether black or white—did not matter. Education was in the estimation of Du Bois, *and* Booker T. Washington among others, the most important tool in the name of political relevance of African Americans. Education remained elusive in terms of discussion—which, to the thinking of both men—likely contributed to the continuation of the difficulties in full realization of an equitable society.

The dozens of books dealing with various aspects of Du Bois' life and work that have been published since the second installment of David Levering Lewis' Pulitzer Prize winning biography was released in 2000 give testament to the renewed interest in the life, words and work of W.E.B. Du Bois. Each of the new books, whether edited compilations or monographs, provide critical examination and offer fresh perspective to the interpretation

Video Sidebar

Education is the best way to empower disenfranchised people.

http://youtu.be/M9_ThOgbLUg

of Du Bois' work. *Education and Empowerment* provides rare examination to the expanse of Du Bois' work as a contributor to educational thought. The seeming lack of exposure begs the inevitable question: does Du Bois' educational thought remain viable and relevant to contemporary education? I believe that the writings contained in this volume prove this to be the case.

Du Bois as an educational thinker is relevant today because many of the core issues he confronted persist today. The role of education as a means by which enlightened citizenship can be gained, an issue addressed in his first writings for public consumption 130 years ago, is still being debated today. The troubling trend of re-segregation of public schools is an issue addressed by Du Bois in his 1935 essay "Does the Negro Need Separate Schools." That essay also addresses issues of multicultural diversity, a buzz word in contemporary educational circles. In the final work included in this volume, "The Talented Tenth: Re-examination of a Concept," Du Bois expresses his disappointment in the African American intellectual elite, and seeks to re-define the role, in hopes of re-invigorating African American leadership.

Du Bois' last three major works, collectively known as the *Black Flame Trilogy*, speaks of the trials of an African American educator who spent much of his life building a college. The final installment, completed in 1961 dealt with issues of the politicization of public colleges.

Du Bois' three historical novels represent the end of a magnificent life in education. Spanning from Reconstruction to *Brown v. Board of Education*, there are more than a few parallels to his life. If there was any segment of his work that merited consideration for inclusion that was *not* included in this volume, it would be these. The difficulty associated with excerpting work from these novels in a way that is consistent with the rest of this book would compromise the literary flow of the trilogy and concomitantly detract from its theme and mission.

Ultimately, Du Bois is relevant as an educator concomitantly because of the timelessness of his message as for the persistence and intractability of the issues confronted. It is my hope that readers of these works will be reminded of the importance of emulating Du Bois in a commitment to the transformative power of education.

Randall Westbrook

SECTION I

MY ILLUSTRIOUS NAME
The Young Du Bois
1883–1885

NEW YORK GLOBE (MAY 3, 1883)

The ladies of the AME Zion Society will hold their monthly supper at the residence of Mrs. L. Gardner on Wednesday[1]. All are invited to attend. There was a large attendance at the Bible Reading last Sunday evening, which was held at Mr. J. Cooley's house. A party came down from Lee [Mass.], Sunday afternoon, and is expected again on Wednesday. The family of Mr. Chinn leave town today for Cleveland, Ohio, including his sister, Mrs. Peterson, who has been visiting them for some time past. Mr. G.F. Jackson will leave the Moore House to go to the Brunswick House at Troy, N.Y. and Mr. C.F. Jackson will succeed him in the culinary department. We are sorry to lose so many colored people[2] from our town but they have "wishes of all." At last week's Sewing Society it was proposed by some to form a literary society but there was not much interest manifested. It would be the best thing that could be done for the colored people if such a society could be formed here.

NEW YORK GLOBE (JUNE 30, 1883)

The ladies of the A.M.E. Zion Church will hold their monthly supper at Mrs. J. Moore's. After the supper there will be a debate on the following question: "Ought the Indian to have been driven out of America?" Messrs. Crosby and Du Bois will take part in

---

1 Du Bois spent much of his time being around members of the African Methodist Episcopal Zion Church in Great Barrington, apparently the social hub for the town's African American community. It's curious how often Du Bois mentions the Sewing Circle, as most of the membership is likely much older, and almost certainly, almost entirely composed of women.
2 Throughout the book, the words "colored" "Negro" "Black" and "African American" will be used interchangeably, based on how Du Bois used them in his writings.

the discussion. Mrs. Sarah Corning, commonly known as "Aunt Sarah," aged 84 years, left town yesterday after a residence of many years, to take up her abode with her daughters at Newport [Rhode Island]. Mr. John Ferries, who has long been an applicant for a pension, has at length received over twelve hundred dollars as back pay to Joseph Smith, of Norfolk, Conn., was visiting friends in town last week. The family of Mr. Chinn, who went West in the Spring, returned here last week.

LETTER TO MOTHER, MARY SILVINA BURGHARDT (1883)

New Bedford [Mass.][3] July 21, 1883

Dear Mam,

I arrived here safely Friday after noon. It was just noon when I got to Hartford. After eating my lunch & buying my ticket I went up to the capitol which is but a little ways to the depot. The grounds are laid out beautifully and the building is magnificent. It consists of a main part and two wings. The main part is surmounted by a tower & dome, which, by the way, is gilded, & upon this is a bronzed statue. As you go in the main entrance the first thing you see is a very large statue of a woman holding a wreath. On either side in cabinets are the different flags. The floor is of colored marble. The staircases are also of marble. There is a book to write your names there & of course my illustrious name is there. I looked into the chamber of the House of representatives. It is very nice. The chairs & desks are arranged in a semicircle. The chairmans[sic] seat is in the middle. In front are seats for the clerks

---

3   This letter was Du Bois' account of his first and only visit to his paternal grandparents. The detail he provides was a familiar vehicle he used in letters to his mother, who by this time was sickly and largely immobile.

& at the side for reporters. There is an elevator which anybody can go up & down in when they wish to. The whole building is frescoed splendidly. On the outside there are niches for statues. There is a picture gallery in the state library room. I cannot tell you ½ what I saw there. I did not go up in dome fearing that the train would leave me. When I came down to the depot & finding that I had a little time left I took a walk up a street near by. When I got back to the depot the train was gone, & news agent told me there was no other to Providence that afternoon. Imagine my situation! At last however I found out there was another train out on another road. So I had to sell my ticket which I paid $2.70 for, for $1.50 because I had my baggage checked on it & baggage had gone by the other train. At last, I was on the way to providence [sic]. The railroad runs down parallel with the Connecticut River & the scenery is beautiful. I saw two or three steamers. After we had got to the coast I changed cars & took the shore line. There the scenery was magnificent the steamers, sailboat, the beautiful seaside resorts & I reached Providence about 8 pm. & there was no one to meet me, Sarah thinking that I would not come because I did not come on the other train I asked a policeman & he directed me to her residence. Providence is a very nice city & I like it very much.

I went around a good deal what little time I was there.

Sarah has a very nice little cottage. I saw the soldiers monument & I will tell you about it when I come. I started on the 8 A.M. train for N.B. [New Bedford] & arrive there about 11 A.M. There was no one to meet me & I was mad, very mad. In fact if I could got hold of some one I should have hurt them, but I didn't. By inquiries I found the house which is about half a mile from the depot. The house is white with green blinds & the yard is full of flower gardens. Grandma is about my color & taller than I thought. I like her very much. Grandpa is short & rather thick set. I like him better than I thought I would. He say very little but speaks civilly when I say anything to him. Grandma says by and bye he'll talk more. I like it very much here & am having a nice time.[4]

Last night Grandma & I took a walk up street & visited some of her friends. I have been walking out this afternoon. We are going on a picnic to onset point next week & down to Martha's Vineyard & to hear the Miss Davis the elocutionist &c.[5] I have not been to Mr. Freedom's yet but will go next week. Tell Jennie not to forget the courier. Tell Grace I would like to slap her once I suppose you are very lonesome. I felt a little home sick this afternoon.

Will write soon, with love to all, good by
Your son,
WE Du Bois

Following his return from New Bedford, Massachusetts, Du Bois used the opportunity, not to talk about his trip, but to further validate his belief in the power of literacy and political engagement for African Americans.

NEW YORK GLOBE (SEPTEMBER 3, 1883)

Your correspondent having been away on vacation no items have appeared for sometime. During my trip I visited Providence, New Bedford, and Albany, and was pleased to see the industry and wealth of many of our race. But one thing that struck me very

---

4   It can be read into Du Bois' account that his grandfather struggled to get used to entertaining his young grandson. There is no indication that the two talked about Du Bois' long absent father who according to records lived less than 10 miles away from his son.

5   Henrietta Vinton Davis (1860–1941) was an African American orator who was a protégée of Frederick Douglass. During the summer of 1883, she toured New England and the Middle Atlantic regions in a rather celebrated tour. Du Bois went to see her in Martha's Vineyard, but she appeared in New Bedford—albeit after Du Bois departed.

forcibly was the absence of literary societies, none of which did I meet in any of the cities. It seems to me as if this of all things ought not to be neglected.

The weather is growing cold here now and it seems as if winter is near at hand.

A singing school has been organized here with Mrs. J. McKinsly as leader. The class meets next Thursday at Mr. Mason's.

On Thursday, Aug. 23, the A.M.E. Zion sewing circle took a ride to Lake Buel. On account of its storming in the early part of the evening a great many who intended, did not go, but those who did reported a very enjoyable time.

Mrs. F. Portland of New York is the guest of Mr. Wm. Crosley. Mr. Egbert Lee took his departure for Springfield last week to attend the Masonic lodge of which he is a member.

There is to be a debate soon before the sewing society upon the question "Should Indians be educated at Hampton?" Messrs. Cooley and Du Bois, affirmative, Messrs. Mason and Crosley, negative. A lively time is expected.

Mr. Wm. Chinn departs Saturday next for Washington, his former home. Your correspondent was pleasantly surprised upon his return, at having his subscription list for *The Globe* doubled through the exertions of Mr. Crosley, who kindly consented to distribute them during his absence and to whom he wishes to return thanks.

Mrs. A. Thompson and daughter of Amherst, Mass., and Mrs. L. Brown of Providence, R.I., arrived today as' guests of Mrs. L. Sumea. The Rev. James Anderson also of Providence is expected here to preach sometime this month. Mr. John Williams, who has been quite sick, has recovered.

New York Globe (September 29, 1883)

The political contest is near at hand, and the colored men of the town should prepare themselves accordingly. They should acquaint themselves with the political status and attitude of the candidates toward them, particularly their representatives. The choice of Governor should also demand a good share of their attention. Those who voted for Gen. Butler last year "just to see what he would do," have found it a pretty costly experiment. They will see that while preaching economy and refusing the necessary appropriations to charitable institutions, he has spent an immense sum of money on needless investigations, such as Tewksbury[6] and the like. The colored men may well ask themselves how they have been benefitted by his administration, although he professes to be their friend.

A political office should not be the goal of one's ambitions, but still if anyone wishes an office and is worthy of it, it should not be denied him on account of his color. We had an example of this here a short time ago, when a colored man, along with a number of white men, applied for the position of night watchman. After an examination the applicants melted down to one white man, a strong Democrat, and the colored man, a Republican. A committee, composed wholly of Republicans was chosen to decide between the two candidates, and they selected the white man.

The colored men of Great Barrington hold the balance of power, and have decided the election of many officers for a number of years. If they will only act in concert they may become a power not to be despised. It would be a good plan if they should meet and decide which way would be most advantageous for them to cast their votes.

---

6   Under the administration of Governor Benjamin Franklin Butler (1883–84), a state hospital in Tewksbury, Massachusetts was built using a controversial amount of state funds.

The debate which I spoke of in my last letter took place last Wednesday evening at the house of Mr. William Crosley. It was contested warmly on both sides and strong arguments were brought up. It was finally decided in favor of the affirmative.[7] After the debate the ladies of Zion Church held their monthly supper.

Mr. Wm. Chinn has returned from Washington. The First Congregational Church, which was dedicated here last Friday, is the handsomest church in the county, and compares with any in the State. The organ, which was given by Mr. Timothy Hopkins of San Francisco, is one of the most complete in the world.

Miss Francis Newport has returned from Pittsfield, where she has been during the Summer. Miss Hattie Sumea returned to Providence last Tuesday. Mr. R. Hines and wife of Norfolk, Conn., were visiting friends in town last week. Mr. William Adams of Hartford, Conn., stopped here a short time and departed for Petersburg, Va. last Thursday. Messrs. Cooley and Mason will have an eating house at the Agricultural Fair, which is held here the 26th, 27th, and 28th inst.

NEW YORK FREEMAN (FEBRUARY 28, 1885)

Surprise parties have been in order during the last few weeks, Mrs. A. W. Austin and Mesdames Newport and Gardner having been visited. Friday evening, the 20th inst., the ladies of Zion Church gave a dime sociable at the house of W. M. Crosley. There was a large attendance and the time most pleasantly passed.

The Sons of Freedom met at the home of the president last evening and elected officers for the ensuing six weeks. Messrs. J. T. Burghardt and W. H. Gardner were elected president and vice. The club will give a short entertainment Monday evening, March 2, for the benefit of the ladies at the residence of Mrs. Newport and Mrs. Gardner. The question, "Which is of the more use to a

---

7   Du Bois' "team" lost the debate.

19

country, the Warrior, the Statesman or the Poet?" will be debated by M. F. Mason, A. W. Austin and W. E. Du Bois.

Mrs. J. Cooley and Mrs. J. Bowen have been visiting friends in New York and Brooklyn recently. Mr. W. M. Crosley met with what might have been a serious accident from the explosion of coal gas two weeks ago. His eyes were injured, but are now better. Mrs. S. Smith of Norfolk, Conn., is the guest of Mrs. D. Brown. Many of the colored people will change their abodes this Spring.

New York Freeman (March 14, 1885)

Miss Julia Newport, the Amherst correspondent of *The Freeman*, was in town a few weeks ago. The open entertainment given by the Sons of Freedom on the evening of the 2nd inst., was greatly enjoyed by all present. The debate, "Which is the most beneficial to a Country the Warrior, Statesman or Poet," was decided in favor of the statesman, whose cause was championed by Mr. A. W. Austin.[8]

Last Friday night a surprise party from this place took a sleigh ride to Sheffield and visited Mr. William Piper. There were about thirty present and festivities were continued until an early hour. Mrs. Piper and daughter are capital hostesses, and we feel like visiting them again. Mr. William L. Chinn is elated at a recent female addition to his household.

The badges which the Sons of Freedom wear on dress occasions were the gifts of Miss Francis Newport. Mrs. R. Williams and son went to Clayton, Conn. last week, to stop a while. Mrs. Josie Bowen returned from Brooklyn last week, but is not yet well enough to be around. Mr. George Wooster of Canaan, Conn has been visiting his daughter, Mrs. J. H. Jackson, but was called home today by the death of his youngest daughter. Miss Grace Freeman has been visiting her parents in Canaan for a few days.

---

8 Du Bois' "team" won the debate.

SECTION II

AND THUS TO RAISE MY RACE
Becoming W.E.B. Du Bois
1885–1903

Westbrook describes the second section of this book which covers the academic life of W.E.B Du Bois, the correspondence with Rutherford B. Hayes, the completion of his Ph.D. and writing *The Souls of Black Folk.*

http://youtu.be/1upOyppgciQ

Letter to Rutherford B. Hayes (1890)

Cambridge, November 4, 1890

Dear Sir:

The following clipping from *The Boston Herald* of Nov. 2nd, has come to my notice:[9]

Negroes in the South

Ex-President Hayes Says Their Chief and Almost Only Gift Is Oratory

Baltimore, Md., Nov. I, 1890, Ex-President Hayes said today to the students of Johns Hopkins University, on the subject of negro education in the South: If there is any young colored man in the South whom we find to have a talent for art or literature, or any especial aptitude for study, we are willing to give him money from the education funds to send him to Europe or to give him an advanced education, but hitherto their chief and almost only gift has been that of oratory.

What you find as historical students, as to their condition in the South, especially in the black belt, is surely not encouraging. They are seen most favorably in what is called the Virginia land district of Ohio. This tract of land, between the Scioto, Little Miami and Ohio rivers, was granted by the state of Virginia to its officers in the revolutionary war, many of whom settled there with their slaves. Most of these were freed, and have increased rapidly with a corresponding increase in education. A careful examination of that region will show a considerable advance in the good qualities of civilization, and proper appreciation of citizenship.

But I do not despair of the other negroes, but am rather hopeful of their being uplifted in the future.

---

9   Clipping from the *Boston Herald* was attached to the original letter.

If this be a true report of your words, I wish to lay my case before you.

I am a Negro, twenty-three years of age next February (23d), and a graduate of Fisk University, '88. After leaving there I came to Harvard University and entering the Junior class graduated in 1890. This year I have entered the graduate School and am a candidate for the degrees of A.M. and Ph.D. in Political Science. I have so far gained my education by teaching in the South, giving small lectures in the North, working in Hotels, laundries, &c, and by various scholarships and the charity of friends. I have no money or property myself and am an orphan. My particular field in Political Science is the History of African Slavery from the economic and social stand point. The faculty of Harvard College have seen fit to recognize whatever ability I have by appointing me to Price Greenleaf aid, a Mathews Scholarship and finally for the year 1890–90 [sic]to a fellowship. For further information as to my character and fitness for my line of work, I respectfully refer to the following gentlemen with whom you may communicate or whose opinion I can procure and forward you:

President Eliot, of Harvard Univ.
Prof. N. S. Shaler,   "   "
Prof. F. G. Peabody,   "   "
Prof. Wm. James,   "   "
Prof. A. B. Hart,   "   "
Prof. T. W. Taussig,   "   "
Frank Bolles, Esq., Sec. Harvard Coll
President E. M. Cravath, Fisk Univ.
Prof. F. A. Chase,   "   "

President F. A. Hosmer, Oahu College, Honolulu, H.I. or the Dean of the Graduate School, Harvard Univ.

If it appears to you upon investigation that I show "any especial aptitude for study," I respectfully ask that I be sent to Europe to pursue my work in the continental universities, leaving the details of the work to the recommendations of the appropriate professors in Harvard.

If the extract above is not correct I pray you will pardon my trespassing.

Respectfully Yours,

W.E.B. Du Bois

LETTER TO RUTHERFORD B. HAYES (1890–1891)

Cambridge, April 19, 1891[10]

Dear Sir:

You will have received by the time this reaches you, I think, testimonials from President Eliot, Prof. Shaler, Prof. Hart, and Prof. Peabody, of Harvard.

I will give you a brief statement of my case.

I was born in Great Barrington, Berkshire County, Mass., on the 23rd Feb. 1868. My grandparents, on my mother's side, were slaves among the Dutch in New York, on my father's side, among the French in the West Indies. I was educated in the public schools of the town; I supported myself and partially supported my mother during my course thro' the High school (father having died when

---

10   This letter was originally dated erroneously as April 19, 1890, one year *before* the letter was actually written.

I was quite young) graduating there in June 1884.[11] I went South to Fisk University in Nashville Tenn. on the recommendation of Rev. C. C. Painter of the Indian Bureau (to whom I am well known) in September 1885. Here I entered the Sophomore class and graduated in June 1888. I was supported while there by the contribution of my own Sunday school in Gt. B. & three others, and by teaching summer schools in the country. In the fall of '88 I secured a Price Greenleaf aid at Harvard and entered the junior class. I supported myself by lectures, loans and prizes. The next year I rec'd a Matthews Scholarship and another prize which with readings delivered during the summer paid my way. I received my degree here in '90 (A.B., cum laude), being one of the Commencement speakers. I then entered the Graduate school to study social science, and was appointed to the Bromfield Rogers Memorial Fellowship. I expect to spend next year here at the same work, after which I wish to spend a couple of years in study in Europe on the same subject.

I am in good physical condition as may be ascertained by the records of the Harvard gymnasium.

I hereby respectfully apply to the board for a fellowship which will enable me to study in Europe one or two years.
Respectfully yours,
W.E.B. Du Bois

P.S. I omitted stating that I am, in blood, about one half or more Negro, and the rest French and Dutch.

---

11   Given Du Bois' training of the time as a historian, his imprecision about information about his parents is rather curious. According to census records, his father, Alfred was very much alive when he graduated high school and likely survived until Du Bois was in his early 60s. Alfred Du Bois was a barber in a neighboring town for several years before and after his son left for Fisk University. Given the closeness of the African American communities in Berkshire County, Massachusetts that persist to the present, it is highly unlikely that Du Bois would not have been aware of his father's presence.

Du Bois received correspondence dated May 2, 1891 from the Slater Fund that while his application was laudable, money previous considered to be available for African Americans to use for study in Europe was no longer available. The ensuing response from Du Bois was terse, direct, and unimaginable from a twenty-two-year-old African American man to a former president of the United States.

LETTER TO RUTHERFORD B. HAYES (1891)

May 25, 1891

Your favor of the 2nd, is at hand. I thank you for your kind wishes. You will pardon me if I add a few words of explanation as to my application. The outcome of the matter is as I expected it would be. The announcement that any agency of the American people was willing to give a Negro a thoroughly liberal education and that it had been looking in vain for men to educate was to say the least rather startling. When the newspaper clipping was handed me in a company of friends, my first impulse was to make in some public way a categorical statement denying that such an offer had ever been made known to colored students. I saw this would be injudicious and fruitless, and I therefore determined on the plan of applying myself. I did so and have been refused along with a number of cases beside mine.

As to my case I personally care little. I am perfectly capable of fighting alone for an education if the trustees do not see fit to help me. On the other hand the injury you have—if unwittingly I trust done the race I represent, and am not ashamed of, is almost irreparable. You went before a number of keenly observant men who looked upon you as an authority in the matter, and told them in substance that the Negroes of the United States either couldn't or wouldn't embrace a most liberal opportunity for advancement. That statement went all over the country. When now finally you receive three or four applications for the fulfillment of that offer, the offer is suddenly withdrawn, while the impression still remains.

If the offer was an experiment, you ought to have had at least one case before withdrawing it; if you have given aid before (and I mean here toward liberal education—not toward training plowmen) then your statement at Johns Hopkins was partial. From the above facts I think you owe an apology to the Negro people. We are ready to furnish competent men for every European scholarship furnished us off paper. But we can't educate ourselves on nothing and we can't have the moral courage to try, if in the midst of our work our friends turn public sentiment against us by making statements which injure us and which they cannot stand by.

That you have been looking for men to liberally educate in the past may be so but it is certainly strange so few have heard it. It was never mentioned during my three years stay at Fisk University. President J.C. Price of Livingstone has told me that he never heard of it, and students from various other Southern schools have expressed great surprise at the offer. The fact is that when I was wanting to come to Harvard, while yet in the South, I wrote to Dr. Haygood for a loan merely, and he never even answered my letter. I find men willing to help me thro' cheap theological schools, I find men willing to help me use my hands before I have got my brains in working order, I have an abundance of good wishes on hand, but I never found a man willing to help me get a Harvard Ph.D. W.E.B. Du Bois

Perhaps to Du Bois' surprise, there was a response—a form of reconsideration that asked him to send more information. And despite his vexation in the previous letter, he complied with the request for additional, clarifying information.

LETTER TO THE TRUSTEES OF THE SLATER FUND (1892)[12]

The Honorable Board of Trustees of the John F. Slater Fund
Gentlemen:

In accordance with your directions I send herewith a sketch of my life.

My name is William Edward Burghardt Du Bois; I was born at Great Barrington, Massachusetts, on the 23rd day of February, 1868, being the sole issue of the marriage of Mary S. Burghardt and Alfred Du Bois. My paternal great-grandfather was a French doctor in the West Indies, and brought my grandfather and his brother to the United States when quite young. My grandfather settled in Connecticut and afterward removed to New Bedford, Mass. He was a boat steward by trade. My father was one of many children, and a barber by trade. He died when I was young.

My mother was a mulatto, the fourth in direct descent from Thomas Burghardt, who when young, was brought from Africa as a slave to the Dutch in New York state, early in the 18th century. He fought in the Revolutionary War. His son Jack Burghardt had several children, among whom was Othello, my grandfather. Othello and his wife, Sally Lampman, were both born slaves, but freed at majority. My mother was the youngest of several children, and received a good common-school education.

Both grandfathers and my father had good common educations. Alexander Du Bois, as my grandfather was named, had accumulated some property, but most of it went to his maintenance in his old age. There was some property in my mother's family but none of it reached me. My father saved nothing; and after his

---

12   Based on Du Bois' reply, this letter was presumably sent in the Spring of 1892.

death we were often near pauperism. Nevertheless my mother kept me in school until she was disabled by paralysis, when I managed to keep on by means of work after hours and on vacation. In 1884 I graduated from the Gt. Barrington High School, and in the fall of 1885 I went south on the advice of friends, and entered the sophomore class at Fisk University. My mother died in the spring of 1885.

I remained at Fisk three years, graduating with the degree of A.B., in 1888. My vacations were spent in teaching country schools. I now determined to come to Harvard and pursue a course for the degree of Ph.D. On the strength of my recommendations I was appointed to $250 of Price Greenleaf Aid at Harvard before coming. During the summer of 1888 I worked in a hotel in the northwest, and in the fall entered the Junior class at this place. I managed to pay the expenses of the first year by the Aid, lecturing, loan fund, and a prize; the next year I was granted a Matthews Scholarship, which added to a series of summer readings and another prize enabled me to finish that year. For the year '90–'91, I was appointed to the H. B. Rogers Memorial Fellowship in Political Science, and re-appointed to the same for 1891–92.

Of the four years spent at Harvard, the first was spent in general studies (e.g. Chemistry, Geology, Ethics, Economics &c), the second year in Philosophy, and Economics; and the last two in History and Political Science. My doctor's thesis has been written and is on the suppression of the slave trade in the United States, including colonial times. My future study will be in political science with especial reference to the history of social problems. Respectfully submitted,
W.E.B. Du Bois

LETTER TO RUTHERFORD B. HAYES (1892)

Cambridge, 3 April '92

Hon. R. B. Hayes
Sir:

I venture with some diffidence to address you again on the subject of a European scholarship from the Slater fund. You expressed the hope, if I remember rightly, that this year the board might see its way more clearly than last year. I wish, therefore, to bring the question to your mind again, and to state my present situation.

At the close of the last academic year at Harvard, I received the degree of master of arts, and was reappointed to my fellowship for the year 1891–92. As it is the general policy of the college to appoint for only two successive years I can have little chance for a third year. My work this year has been the general study of history, sociology &c., and the preparation of my thesis for the doctor's degree, on the suppression of the African Slave Trade in America. A preliminary paper on this subject, I read before the Annual meeting of the American Historical Association, of which I have been made a member. The paper will be shortly published in their proceedings, and a preliminary report may be found in the *Independent*, 7 Jan., '92 (also *Congregationalist* about same date). The thesis itself is now finished in rough draft, and will be ready for publication May 1.

To properly finish the education thus begun, a careful training in a European university for at least a year is, in my mind, and in the minds of my professors, indispensable to my greatest usefulness. I therefore desire to lay three propositions before you:

1. That the board grant me a scholarship from the funds, upon which I may I be enabled to spend a year in study at a European university, under the direction [of] those whom they appoint.

2. If this be impracticable, that the board loan me a sum sufficient for such a purpose. I could only give my note of hand as security for this, but I do not think that such a note would be worthless. I could probably repay the sum within two years after finishing.

3. If neither of the above plans are agreed to by the board, could you or they suggest some person interested enough in the "Negro problem," to make such a loan to me?

In case all these suggestions fail, I would like to ask if you would object to returning to me the recommendations forwarded you in regard to my case (except personal notes) in order that I may use them in other directions for the same purpose.

I trust you will pardon my importunity—I can only say by way of excuse, that I do not consider it is a question of merely personal interest.

Respectfully yours,

W.E.B. Du Bois

Video Sidebar

Westbrook tells the story of how Du Bois convinced former President Rutherford B. Hayes and the John F. Slater Fund to sponsor his studies toward his Ph.D. at the University of Berlin.

http://youtu.be/nyj2An4ek7Y

JOURNAL ENTRY (FEBRUARY 23, 1893)

1868–1893
Berlin, Germany, Oranienstrasse No 130A.
Program for the
Celebration of my twenty-fifth birthday

Birthday-eve

7-9	Music	10$^{1/2}$-12	Letters to Grandma Mabel
9–10½	Plans	12	Sacrifice to the Zeitgeist
			Mercy—God—work

Birthday

7–8–9½	Breakfast–old letters	6–7	Seminar
	Reflection Parents	7–8	Supper (Greek wine,
	Home		cocoa, Kirchen, oranges
	Poetry Steal Away	8–10	Year Book
	Song Jesus Lover of my	10–12	Letters to C.B. Carrington
	Soul		Florence
	America		
9 ½–11	A Wander		
11–1	Art		
1–3	Dinner		
3–6	Coffee in Potsdam		

W.E.B. Du Bois

This programme was very pleasantly carried out. I arose at eight
and took coffee and oranges, read letters, thought of my parents,
sang, cried, etc. (O yes, the night before I heard Schubert's beautiful Unfinished Symphony, planned my celebration and room,
wrote to grandma and Mabel and had a curious…) ceremony with
candle, greek wine, oil, and song and prayer. Then I dedicated
my library to mother. Then I wandered up to the reading room;
then to the art gallery; then to a fine dinner with Einderhof over

a bottle of Rudecheimer and cigarettes. Then went to Potsdam for coffee and saw a pretty girl. Then came back to the Seminar; took a wander, supped on cocoa, wine, oranges and cake; wrote my year book and letters—and now I go to bed after one of the happiest days of my happy life.

Night—grand and wonderful. I am glad I am living. I rejoice as a strong man to run a race, and I am strong—is it egotism—is it assurance—or is [it] the silent call of the world spirit that makes me feel that I am royal and that beneath my sceptre a world of kings shall bow. The hot dark blood of that forefather—born king of men—is beating at my heart, and I know that I am either a genius or a fool. O I wonder what I am—I wonder what the world is—I wonder if Life is worth the striving—I do not know—perhaps I never shall know: but this I do know: be the Truth what it may I will seek it, on the pure assumption that it is worth seeking and Heaven nor Hell: God nor Devil shall turn me from my purpose till I die.

I will in this second quarter century of my life, enter the dark forest of the unknown world for which I have so many years served my apprenticeship—the chart and compass the world furnishes me I have little faith in—yet, I have none better—I will seek till I find—and die. There is grandeur in the very hopelessness of such a life—life? and is life all? If I strive, shall I live to strive again? I do not know and in spite of the wild *sehnsucht* for Eternity that makes my heartsick now and then—I shut my teeth and say I do not care. *Carpe Diem!* What is life but life, after all. Its end is its greatest and fullest self—this end is the Good. The Beautiful its attribute—its soul, and Truth its being. Not three commensurable things are these, they are three dimensions of the cube. Mayhap God is the fourth, but for that very reason incomprehensible. The greatest and fullest life is by definition beautiful, beautiful,—beautiful as a dark passionate woman, beautiful as a golden hearted school girl, beautiful as a grey haired hero. That is the dimension of breadth. Then comes Truth—what is, cold and indisputable: that is height. Now I will, so help my Soul, multiply breadth by breadth, Beauty by Truth and then Goodness, strength, shall bind them together into a solid whole.

Wherefore? I know not now. Perhaps infinite other dimensions do. This is a wretched figure and yet it roughly represents my attitude toward the world. I am striving to make my life all that life may be—and I am limiting that strife only in so far as that strife is incompatible with others of my brothers and sisters making their lives similar. The crucial question now is where that limit comes. I am too often puzzled to know. Paul put it at meat-eating, which was asinine. I have put it at the (perhaps) life-ruin of Amalie which is cruel. God knows I am sorely puzzled. I am firmly convinced that my own best development is now one and the same with the best development of the world and here I am willing to sacrifice. That sacrifice is working for the multiplication of Youth × Beauty and now comes the question how. The general proposition of working for the world's good becomes too soon sickly sentimentality. I therefore take the work that the Unknown lay in my hands and work for the rise of the Negro people, taking for granted that their best development means the best development of the world.

This night before my life's altar I reiterate, what my life...[13]

I remembered how when wandering in the fields I chose the realm of Mind for my territory and planned Harvard and Europe. My loves—O my loves, how many and how dear, she is the beautiful whom I worshipped, Ollie the lonely, Dicky the timid, Jenny the meek, Nellie the wavery child. Then came a commencement when hundreds applauded—Nell carried my diploma—and then I left for the Northwest.[14] Then came Harvard—scholarships, high marks,

---

13   Pages 7-10 are missing from the original manuscript.
14   In describing his years at Fisk University, Du Bois often referred to Tennessee as "west" or "northwest."

Boylston prizes when Cambridge applauded, Commencement when the Harvard applause awoke echoes in the world—then Europe where the heart of my childhood loosed from the hard iron hands of America has beat again in the great inspiring air of world culture. I only know Germany—its Rhine or memories, its München or Gemutlichkeit, its Dresden or Art, its Berlin with its music and militarism. These are the five and twenty years of my apprenticeship.

These are my plans: to make a name in science, to make a name in literature and thus to raise my race. Or perhaps to raise a visible empire in Africa thro' England, France or Germany. I wonder what will be the outcome? Who knows?

I will go unto the king—which is not according to the law and if I perish
—I PERISH.

The following year, in celebrating his 26th birthday, Du Bois again detailed the birthday celebration. The tone however was far different from the previous year. Just days later, he was more likely to be denied, Du Bois wrote to the committee. Interestingly, he mentions former president Hayes who died just before Du Bois' 25th birthday. The inference here is that he had no communication with the Slater Fund for more than a year. It could be conjectured that their concerns were threefold: 1) the potential backlash that could result from financing an African American to become the most credentialed man in America; 2) that Du Bois' lack of communication with the Fund trustees suggested to them that he was engaged in frivolities; 3) that he had not to that point displayed an adequate deference to the Fund—especially in light of his initial correspondence.

LETTER TO THE TRUSTEES OF THE SLATER FUND (1893)

March 1893

To the Honorable,

The Trustees of the John F. Slater Fund

Gentlemen:

I desire to express to you, hereby, my sincerest gratitude for the scholarship which at your last annual meeting you were pleased to grant me. I am especially grateful to the memory of him, your late head, through whose initiative my case was brought before you, and whose tireless energy and singleheartedness for the interests of my Race, God has at last crowned. I shall, believe me, ever strive that these efforts shall not be wholly without result.

The use to which your grant has been put, I have according to agreement laid in the hands of the Educational committee.

In addition to this grant, I feel compelled humbly to petition that a similar grant be made to me for the coming year. It is with the greatest diffidence that I make this request, for I am well aware how manifold and worthy the objects are, for which the fund intrusted to your care is spent. Upon maturest consideration however, I feel in duty bound to make the petition: I do not ask for another year of European study merely because it would be pleasant, but because I regard such a period in the highest degree necessary to the completion of my education. I realize, Gentlemen, the great weight of responsibility that rests upon the younger generation of Negroes, and I feel that, handicapped as I must inevitably be to some extent in the race of life, I cannot afford to start with a preparation a bit poorer or cheaper than that deemed best for the best usefulness of my white fellow-students. To the American Negro even more than to the white, is the contact with

European culture of inestimable value in giving him a broad view of men and affairs, and enabling him to view the problems of his race in their true perspective.

I therefore ask that the Honorable Trustees extend their grant to the coming year to enable me to finish my studies at the University of Berlin and the School of Economics at Paris, under whatever conditions they may see fit to impose.

I am, gentlemen

Your Obedient Servant,

W.E.B. Du Bois

A Negro Schoolmaster in the New South (1899)[15]

Once upon a time I taught school in the hills of Tennessee, where the broad dark vale of the Mississippi begins to roll and crumple to greet the Alleghanies. I was a Fisk student then, and all Fisk men think that Tennessee—beyond the Veil—is theirs alone, and in vacation time they sally forth in lusty bands to meet the country school commissioners. Young and Happy, I too went, and I shall not soon forget that summer, ten years ago.

First, there was a teachers' Institute at the county-seat; and there distinguished guests of the superintendent taught the teachers fractions and spelling and other mysteries,—white teachers in the morning, Negroes at night. A picnic now and then, and a supper, and the rough world was softened by laughter and song. I remember how—But I wander.

There came a day when all the teachers left the Institute, and began the hunt for schools. I learn from hearsay (for my mother was mortally afraid of fire-arms) that the hunting of ducks and

---

15   Originally appeared in *The Atlantic Monthly*, January 1899. A similar version of this essay is later included in *The Souls of Black Folk* under the title "Of the Meaning of Progress."

bears and men is wonderfully interesting, but I am sure that the man who has never hunted a country school has something to learn of the pleasures of the chase. I see now the white, hot roads lazily rise and fall and wind before me under the burning July sun; I feel the deep weariness of heart and limb, as ten, eight, six miles stretch relentlessly ahead; I feel my heart sink heavily as I hear again and again, "Got a teacher? Yes." So I walked on and on,—horses were too expensive,—until I had wandered beyond railways, beyond stage lines, to a land of "varmints" and rattle-snakes, where the coming of a stranger was an event, and men lived and died in the shadow of one blue hill.

Sprinkled over hill and dale lay cabins and farmhouses, shut out from the world by the forests and the rolling hills toward the east. There I found at last a little school. Josie told me of it; she was a thin, homely girl of twenty, with a dark brown face and thick, hard hair. I had crossed the stream at Watertown, and rested under the great willows; then I had gone to the little cabin in the lot where Josie was resting on her way to town. The gaunt farmer made me welcome, and Josie, hearing my errand, told me anxiously that they wanted a school over the hill; that but once since the war had a teacher been there; that she herself longed to learn,—and thus she ran on, talking fast and loud, with much earnestness and energy.

Next morning I crossed the tall round hill, lingered to look at the blue and yellow mountains stretching toward the Carolinas; then I plunged into the wood, and came out at Josie's home. It was a dull frame cottage with four rooms, perched just below the brow of the hill, amid peach trees. The father was a quiet, simple soul, calmly ignorant, with no touch of vulgarity. The mother was different,—strong, bustling, and energetic, with a quick, restless tongue, and an ambition to live "like folks." There was a crowd of children. Two boys had gone away. There remained two growing girls; a shy midget of eight; John, tall, awkward, and eighteen; Jim, younger, quicker, and better looking; and two babies of indefinite age. Then there was Josie herself. She seemed to be the centre of the family: always busy at service or at home, or berry-picking; a little nervous and inclined to scold, like her mother, yet faithful, too, like her father. She had about her a certain fineness, the shadow of an unconscious moral heroism that would willingly give all of life to make life broader, deeper and fuller for her and hers. I saw much of this family afterward, and grew to love them for their honest efforts to be decent and comfortable, and for their knowledge of their own ignorance. There was with them no affectation. The mother would scold the father for being so "easy;" Josie would roundly rate the boys for carelessness; and all knew that it was a hard thing to dig a living out of a rocky side hill.

I secured the school. I remember the day I rode horseback out to the commissioner's house, with a pleasant young white fellow, who wanted the white school. The road ran down the bed of a stream; the sun laughed and the water jingled, and we rode on. "Come in," said the commissioner,—"come in. Have a seat. Yes, that certificate will do. Stay to dinner. What do you want a month?" Oh, thought I, this is lucky; but even then fell the awful shadow of the Veil, for they ate first, then I—alone.

The schoolhouse was a log hut, where Colonel Wheeler used to shelter his corn. It sat in a lot behind a rail fence and thorn bushes, near the sweetest of spring. There was an entrance where a door once was, and within, a massive rickety fireplace; great chinks between the logs served as windows. Furniture was scarce. A pale blackboard crouched in the corner. My desk was made of three boards, reinforced at critical points, and my chair, borrowed from the landlady, had to be returned every night. Seats for the children,– these puzzled me much. I was haunted by a New England vision of neat little desks and chairs, but, alas, the reality was rough plank benches without backs, and at times without legs. They had the one virtue of making naps dangerous, a—possibly fatal, for the floor was not to be trusted.

It was a hot morning late in July when the school opened. I trembled when I heard the patter of little feet down the dusty road, and saw the growing row of dark solemn faces and bright eager eyes facing me. First came Josie and her brothers and sisters. The longing to know, to be a student in the great school at Nashville, hovered like a star above this child woman amid her work and worry, and she studied doggedly. There were the Dowells from their farm over toward Alexandria: Fanny, with her smooth black face and wondering eyes; Martha, brown and dull; the pretty girl wife of a brother, and the younger brood. There were the Burkes, two brown and yellow lads, and tine haughty-eyed girl. Fat Reuben's little chubby girl came, with golden face and old gold hair, faithful and solemn. Thenie was on hand early,—a jolly, ugly, good-hearted girl, who slyly dipped snuff and looked after her little bow-legged brother. When her mother could spare her, 'Tildy came,—a midnight beauty, with starry eyes and tapering limbs; and her brother, correspondingly homely. And then the big boys: the hulking Lawrences; the lazy Neills, unfathered sons of mother and daughter; Hickman, with a stoop in his shoulders; and the rest.

There they sat, nearly thirty of them, on the rough benches, their faces shading from a pale cream to a deep brown, the little feet bare and swinging, the eyes full of expectation, with here and there a twinkle of mischief, and the hands grasping Webster's blue-back spelling-book. I loved my school, and the fine faith the children had in the wisdom of their teacher was truly marvelous. We read and spelled together, wrote a little, picked flowers, sang, and listened to stories of the world beyond the hill. At times the school would dwindle away, and I would start out. I would visit Mun Eddings, who lived in two very dirty rooms, and ask why little Lugene, whose flaming face seemed ever ablaze with the dark red hair uncombed, was absent all last week, or why I missed so often the inimitable rags of Mack and Ed. Then the father, who worked Colonel Wheeler's farm on shares, would tell me how the crops needed the boys; and the thin, slovenly mother, whose face was pretty when washed, assured me that Lugene must mind the baby. "But we'll start them again next week." When the Lawrences stopped, I knew that the doubt of the old folks about book-learning had conquered again, and so, toiling up the hill, and getting as far into the cabin as possible, I put Cicero *pro Archia Poeta*[16] in the simplest English with local applications, and usually convinced them—for a week or so.

On Friday nights I often went home with some of the children; sometimes to Doc Burke's farm. He was a great, loud, thin Black, ever working, and trying to buy the seventy-five acres of hill and dale where he lived; but people said that he would surely fail, and the "white folks would get it all." His wife was a magnificent Amazon, with saffron face and shining hair, uncorseted and barefooted, and the children were strong and beautiful. They lived in a one-and-a half-room cabin in the hollow of the farm, near the spring. The front room was full of great fat white beds, scrupulously neat; and there were bad chromos on the walls, and a tired centre-table. In the tiny back kitchen I was often invited to "take out and help" myself to fried chicken and wheat biscuit, "meat" and corn pone, string beans and berries. At first I used to be a little alarmed at the approach of bedtime in the one lone bedroom, but embarrassment was very deftly avoided. First, all the children nodded and slept, and were stowed away in one great pile of goose feathers; next, the mother and the father discreetly

---

16   Du Bois was fond of the works of Marcus Tulius Cicero (106–43 BC). Cicero's defense of human rights resonated with the young Du Bois and continued to be an influence in his writings for the rest of his life.

slipped away to the kitchen while I went to bed; then, blowing out the dim light, they retired in the dark. In the morning all were up and away before I thought of awakening. Across the road, where fat Reuben lived, they all went outdoors while the teacher retired, because they did not boast the luxury of a kitchen.

I liked to stay with the Dowells, for they had four rooms and plenty of good country fare. Uncle Bird had a small, rough farm, all woods and hills, miles from the big road; but he was full of tales,—he preached now and then,—and with his children, berries, horses, and wheat he was happy and prosperous. Often, to keep the peace, I must go where life was less lovely; for instance, 'Tildy's mother was incorrigibly dirty, Reuben's larder was limited seriously, and herds of untamed bedbugs wandered over the Eddingses' beds. Best of all I loved to go to Josie's, and sit on the porch, eating peaches, while the mother bustled and talked: how Josie had bought the sewing-machine; how Josie worked at service in winter, but that four dollars a month was "mighty little" wages; how Josie longed to go away to school, but that it "looked like" they never could get far enough ahead to let her; how the crops failed and the well was yet unfinished; and, finally, how "mean" some of the white folks were.

For two summers I lived in this little world; it was dull and humdrum. The girls looked at the hill in wistful longing, and the boys fretted, and haunted Alexandria. Alexandria was "town,"— a straggling, lazy village of houses, churches, and shops, and an aristocracy of Toms, Dicks, and Captains. Cuddled on the hill to the north was the village of the colored folks, who lived in three or four room unpainted cottages, some neat and homelike, and some dirty. The dwellings were scattered rather aimlessly, but they centred about the twin temples of the hamlet, the Methodist and the Hard-Shell Baptist churches. These, in turn, leaned gingerly on a sad-colored schoolhouse. Hither my little world wended its crooked way on Sunday to meet other worlds, and gossip, and wonder, and make the weekly sacrifice with frenzied priest at the altar of the "old-time religion." Then the soft melody and mighty cadences of Negro song fluttered and thundered.

I have called my tiny community a world, and so its isolation made it; and yet there was among us but a half-awakened common consciousness, sprung from common joy and grief, at burial, birth, or wedding; from a common hardship in poverty, poor land, and low wages; and, above all, from the sight of the Veil that hung between us and Opportunity. All this caused us to think some thoughts together; but these, when ripe for speech, were spoken in various languages. Those whose eyes thirty and more years before had seen "the glory of the coming of the Lord" saw in every present hindrance or help a dark fatalism bound to bring all things right in His own good time. The mass of those to whom slavery was a dim recollection of childhood found the world a puzzling thing: it asked little of them, and they answered with little, and yet it ridiculed their offering. Such a paradox they could not understand, and therefore sank into listless indifference, or shiftlessness, or reckless bravado. There were, however, some such as Josie, Jim, and Ben,—they to whom War, Hell, and Slavery were but childhood tales, whose young appetites had been whetted to an edge by school and story and half-awakened thought. Ill could they be content, born without and beyond the World. And their weak wings beat against their barriers,—barriers of caste, of youth, of life; at last, in dangerous moments, against everything that opposed even a whim.

The ten years that follow youth, the years when first the realization comes that life is leading somewhere,—these were the years that passed after I left my little school. When they were past, I came by chance once more to the walls of Fisk University, to the halls of the chapel of melody. As I lingered there in the joy and pain of meeting old school friends, there swept over me a sudden longing to pass again beyond the blue hill, and to see the homes and the school of other days, and to learn how life had gone with my school-children; and I went.

Josie was dead, and the gray-haired mother said simply, "We've had a heap of trouble since you've been away." I had feared for Jim. With a cultured parentage and a social caste to uphold him, he might have made a venturesome merchant or a West Point cadet. But here he was, angry with life and reckless; and when Farmer Durham charged him with stealing wheat, the old man had to ride fast to escape the stones which the furious fool hurled after him. They told Jim to run away; but he would not run, and the constable came that afternoon. It grieved Josie, and great awkward John walked nine miles every day to see his little brother through the bars of Lebanon jail. At last the two came back together in the dark night. The mother cooked supper, and Josie emptied her purse, and the boys stole away. Josie grew thin and silent, yet worked the more. The hill became steep for the quiet old father, and with the boys away there was little to do in the valley. Josie helped them sell the old farm, and they moved nearer town. Brother Dennis, the carpenter, built a new house with six rooms; Josie toiled a year in Nashville, and brought back ninety dollars to furnish the house and change it to a home.

When the spring came, and the birds twittered, and the stream ran proud and full, little sister Lizzie, bold and thoughtless, flushed with the passion of youth, bestowed herself on the tempter, and brought home a nameless child. Josie shivered, and worked on, with the vision of schooldays all fled, with a face wan and tired,— worked until, on a summer's day, some one married another; then Josie crept to her mother like a hurt child, and slept—and sleeps.

I paused to scent the breeze as I entered the valley. The Lawrences have gone; father and son forever, and the other son lazily digs in the earth to live. A new young widow rents out their cabin to fat Reuben. Reuben is a Baptist preacher now, but I fear as lazy as ever, though his cabin has three rooms; and little Ella has grown into a bouncing woman, and is ploughing corn on the hot hillside. There are babies a plenty, and one half-witted girl. Across the valley is a house I did not know before, and there I found, rocking one baby and expecting another, one of my schoolgirls, a daughter of Uncle Bird Dowell. She looked somewhat worried with her new duties, but soon bristled into pride over her neat cabin, and the tale of her thrifty husband, the horse and cow, and farm they were planning to buy.

My log schoolhouse was gone. In its place stood Progress, and Progress, I understand, is necessarily ugly. The crazy foundation stones still marked the former site of my poor little cabin, and not far away, on six weary boulders, perched a jaunty board house, perhaps twenty by thirty feet, with three windows and a door that locked. Some of the window glass was broken, and part of an old iron stove lay mournfully under the house. I peeped through the window half reverently, and found things that were more familiar. The blackboard had grown by about two feet, and the seats were still without backs. The county owns the lot now, I hear, and every year there is a session of school. As I sat by the spring and looked on the Old and the New I felt glad, very glad, and yet—

After two long drinks I started on. There was the great double log house on the corner. I remembered the broken, blighted family that used to live there. The strong, hard face of the mother, with its wilderness of hair, rose before me. She had driven her husband away, and while I taught school a strange man lived there, big and jovial, and people talked. I felt sure that Ben and 'Tildy would come to naught from such a home. But this is an odd world; for Ben is a busy farmer in Smith County, "doing well, too," they say, and he had cared for little 'Tildy until last spring, when a lover married her. A hard life the lad had led, toiling for meat, and laughed at because he was homely and crooked. There was Sam Carlton, an impudent old skinflint, who had definite notions about niggers, and hired Ben a summer and would not pay him. Then the hungry boy gathered his sacks together, and in broad daylight went into Carlton's corn; and when the hard-fisted farmer set upon him, the angry boy flew at him like a beast. Doc Burke saved a murder and a lynching that day.

The story reminded me again of the Burkes, and an impatience seized me to know who won in the battle, Doc or the seventy-five acres. For it is a hard thing to make a farm out of nothing, even in fifteen years. So I hurried on, thinking of the Burkes. They used to have a certain magnificent barbarism about them that I liked. "They were never vulgar, never immoral, but rather rough and primitive, with an unconventionality that spent itself in loud guffaws, slaps on the back, and naps in the corner. I hurried by the cottage of the misborn Neill boys. It was empty, and they were grown into fat, lazy farm hands. I saw the home of the Hickmans, but Albert, with his stooping shoulders, had passed from the world. Then I came to the Burkes' gate and peered through; the inclosure looked rough and untrimmed, and yet there were the same fences around the old farm save to the left, where lay twenty five other acres. And lo! the cabin in the hollow had climbed the hill and swollen to a half-finished six-room cottage.

The Burkes held a hundred acres, but they were still in debt. Indeed, the gaunt father who toiled night and day would scarcely be happy out of debt, being so used to it. Some day he must stop, for his massive frame is showing decline. The mother wore shoes, but the lion-like physique of other days was broken. The children had grown up. Rob, the image of his father, was loud and rough with laughter. Birdie, my school baby of six, had grown to a picture of maiden beauty, tall and tawny. "Edgar is gone," said the mother, with head half bowed, "—gone to work in Nashville; he and his father couldn't agree."

47

Little Doc, the boy born since the time of my school, took me horseback down the creek next morning toward Farmer Dowell's. The road and the stream were battling for mastery, and the stream had the better of it. We splashed and waded, and the merry boy, perched behind me, chattered and laughed. He showed me where Simon Thomspon had bought a bit of ground and a home; but his daughter Lana, a plump, brown, slow girl, was not there. She had married a man with a farm twenty miles away. We wound on down the stream till we came to a gate that I did not recognize, but the boy insisted that it was "Uncle Bird's." The farm was fat with the growing crop. In that little valley was a strange stillness as I rode up; for death and marriage had stolen youth, and left age and childhood there. We sat and talked that night, after the chores were done. Uncle Bird was grayer, and his eyes did not see so well, but he was still jovial. We talked of acres bought,—one hundred and twenty-five,—of the new guest, chamber added, of Martha's marrying. Then we talked of death: Fanny and Fred were gone; a shadow hung over the other daughter, and when it lifted she was to go to Nashville to school. At last we spoke of the neighbors, and as night fell Uncle Bird told me how, on a night like that, 'Thenie came wandering back to her home over yonder, to escape the blows of her husband. And next morning she died in the home that her little bow-legged brother, working and saving, had bought for their widowed mother.

My journey was done, and behind me lay hill and dale, and Life and Death. How shall man measure Progress there where the dark-faced Josie lies? How many heartfuls of sorrow shall balance a bushel of wheat? How hard a thing is life to the lowly, and yet how human and real! And all this life and love and strife and failure,—is it the twilight of nightfall or the flush of some faint-dawning day?

Thus sadly musing, I rode to Nashville in the Jim Crow car.

OF MR. BOOKER T. WASHINGTON AND OTHERS (1903)[17]

From birth till death enslaved; in word, in deed, unmanned!

* * * * * *

Hereditary bondsmen! Know ye not
Who would be free themselves must strike the blow?

—BYRON

Easily the most striking thing in the history of the American Negro since 1876 is the ascendancy of Mr. Booker T. Washington. It began at the time when war memories and ideals were rapidly passing; a day of astonishing commercial development was dawning; a sense of doubt and hesitation overtook the freedmen's sons,—then it was that his leading began. Mr. Washington came, with a simple definite programme, at the psychological moment when the nation was a little ashamed of having bestowed so much sentiment on Negroes, and was concentrating its energies on Dollars. His programme of industrial education, conciliation of the South, and submission and silence as to civil and political rights, was not wholly original; the Free Negroes from 1830 up to war-time had striven to build industrial schools, and the American Missionary Association had from the first taught various trades; and Price and others had sought a way of honorable alliance with the best of the Southerners. But Mr. Washington first indissolubly linked these things; he put enthusiasm, unlimited energy, and perfect faith into his programme, and changed it from a by-path into a veritable Way of Life. And the tale of the methods by which he did this is a fascinating study of human life.

It startled the nation to hear a Negro advocating such a programme after many decades of bitter complaint; it startled and

---

17   Originally appeared in *The Souls of Black Folk*, A.C. McClurg & Co. 1903.

won the applause of the South, it interested and won the admiration of the North; and after a confused murmur of protest, it silenced if it did not convert the Negroes themselves.

To gain the sympathy and cooperation of the various elements comprising the white South was Mr. Washington's first task; and this, at the time Tuskegee was founded, seemed, for a black man, well-nigh impossible. And yet ten years later it was done in the word spoken at Atlanta: "In all things purely social we can be as separate as the five fingers, and yet one as the hand in all things essential to mutual progress." This "Atlanta Compromise" is by all odds the most notable thing in Mr. Washington's career. The South interpreted it in different ways: the radicals received it as a complete surrender of the demand for civil and political equality; the conservatives, as a generously conceived working basis for mutual understanding. So both approved it, and to-day its author is certainly the most distinguished Southerner since Jefferson Davis, and the one with the largest personal following.

Next to this achievement comes Mr. Washington's work in gaining place and consideration in the North. Others less shrewd and tactful had formerly essayed to sit on these two stools and had fallen between them; but as Mr. Washington knew the heart of the South from birth and training, so by singular insight he intuitively grasped the spirit of the age which was dominating the North. And so thoroughly did he learn the speech and thought of triumphant commercialism, and the ideals of material prosperity, that the picture of a lone black boy poring over a French grammar amid the weeds and dirt of a neglected home soon seemed to him the acme of absurdities. One wonders what Socrates and St. Francis of Assisi would say to this.

And yet this very singleness of vision and thorough oneness with his age is a mark of the successful man. It is as though Nature must needs make men narrow in order to give them force. So Mr.

Washington's cult has gained unquestioning followers, his work has wonderfully prospered, his friends are legion, and his enemies are confounded. To-day he stands as the one recognized spokesman of his ten million fellows, and one of the most notable figures in a nation of seventy millions. One hesitates, therefore, to criticise a life which, beginning with so little, has done so much. And yet the time is come when one may speak in all sincerity and utter courtesy of the mistakes and shortcomings of Mr. Washington's career, as well as of his triumphs, without being thought captious or envious, and without forgetting that it is easier to do ill than well in the world.

The criticism that has hitherto met Mr. Washington has not always been of this broad character. In the South especially has he had to walk warily to avoid the harshest judgments,—and naturally so, for he is dealing with the one subject of deepest sensitiveness to that section. Twice—once when at the Chicago celebration of the Spanish-American War he alluded to the color-prejudice that is "eating away the vitals of the South," and once when he dined with President Roosevelt—has the resulting Southern criticism been violent enough to threaten seriously his popularity. In the North the feeling has several times forced itself into words, that Mr. Washington's counsels of submission overlooked certain elements of true manhood, and that his educational programme was unnecessarily narrow. Usually, however, such criticism has not found open expression, although, too, the spiritual sons of the Abolitionists have not been prepared to acknowledge that the schools founded before Tuskegee, by men of broad ideals and self-sacrificing spirit, were wholly failures or worthy of ridicule. While, then, criticism has not failed to follow Mr. Washington, yet the prevailing public opinion of the land has been but too willing to deliver the solution of a wearisome problem into his hands, and say, "If that is all you and your race ask, take it."

51

Among his own people, however, Mr. Washington has encountered the strongest and most lasting opposition, amounting at times to bitterness, and even today continuing strong and insistent even though largely silenced in outward expression by the public opinion of the nation. Some of this opposition is, of course, mere envy; the disappointment of displaced demagogues and the spite of narrow minds. But aside from this, there is among educated and thoughtful colored men in all parts of the land a feeling of deep regret, sorrow, and apprehension at the wide currency and ascendancy which some of Mr. Washington's theories have gained. These same men admire his sincerity of purpose, and are willing to forgive much to honest endeavor which is doing something worth the doing. They cooperate with Mr. Washington as far as they conscientiously can; and, indeed, it is no ordinary tribute to this man's tact and power that, steering as he must between so many diverse interests and opinions, he so largely retains the respect of all.

But the hushing of the criticism of honest opponents is a dangerous thing. It leads some of the best of the critics to unfortunate silence and paralysis of effort, and others to burst into speech so passionately and intemperately as to lose listeners. Honest and earnest criticism from those whose interests are most nearly touched,—criticism of writers by readers,—this is the soul of democracy and the safeguard of modern society. If the best of the American Negroes receive by outer pressure a leader whom they had not recognized before, manifestly there is here a certain palpable gain. Yet there is also irreparable loss,—a loss of that peculiarly valuable education which a group receives when by search and criticism it finds and commissions its own leaders. The way in which this is done is at once the most elementary and the nicest problem of social growth. History is but the record of such group-leadership; and yet how infinitely changeful is its type and character! And of all types and kinds, what can be more instructive than the leadership of a group within a group?—that curious double movement where real progress may be negative and actual advance be relative retrogression. All this is the social student's inspiration and despair.

Now in the past the American Negro has had instructive experience in the choosing of group leaders, founding thus a peculiar dynasty which in the light of present conditions is worth while studying. When sticks and stones and beasts form the sole environment of a people, their attitude is largely one of determined opposition to and conquest of natural forces. But when to earth and brute is added an environment of men and ideas, then the attitude of the imprisoned group may take three main forms,—a feeling of revolt and revenge; an attempt to adjust all thought and action to the will of the greater group; or, finally, a determined effort at self-realization and self-development despite environing opinion. The influence of all of these attitudes at various times can be traced in the history of the American Negro, and in the evolution of his successive leaders.

Before 1750, while the fire of African freedom still burned in the veins of the slaves, there was in all leadership or attempted leadership but the one motive of revolt and revenge,—typified in the terrible Maroons, the Danish blacks, and Cato of Stono, and veiling all the Americas in fear of insurrection. The liberalizing tendencies of the latter half of the eighteenth century brought, along with kindlier relations between black and white, thoughts of ultimate adjustment and assimilation. Such aspiration was especially voiced in the earnest songs of Phyllis, in the martyrdom of Attucks, the fighting of Salem and Poor, the intellectual accomplishments of Banneker and Derham, and the political demands of the Cuffes.

Stern financial and social stress after the war cooled much of the previous humanitarian ardor. The disappointment and impatience of the Negroes at the persistence of slavery and serfdom voiced itself in two movements. The slaves in the South, aroused undoubtedly by vague rumors of the Haytian revolt, made three fierce attempts at insurrection,—in 1800 under Gabriel in Virginia, in 1822 under Vesey in Carolina, and in 1831 again in Virginia under the terrible Nat Turner. In the Free States, on the other hand, a new and curious attempt at self-development was made. In Philadelphia and New York color-prescription led to a withdrawal of Negro communicants from white churches and the formation of a peculiar socio-religious institution among the Negroes known as the African Church,—an organization still living and controlling in its various branches over a million of men.

Walker's wild appeal against the trend of the times showed how the world was changing after the coming of the cotton-gin. By 1830 slavery seemed hopelessly fastened on the South, and the slaves thoroughly cowed into submission. The free Negroes of the North, inspired by the mulatto immigrants from the West Indies, began to change the basis of their demands; they recognized the slavery of slaves, but insisted that they themselves were freemen, and sought assimilation and amalgamation with the nation on the same terms with other men. Thus, Forten and Purvis of Philadelphia, Shad of Wilmington, Du Bois of New Haven, Barbadoes of Boston, and others, strove singly and together as men, they said, not as slaves; as "people of color," not as "Negroes." The trend of the times, however, refused them recognition save in individual and exceptional cases, considered them as one with all the despised blacks, and they soon found themselves striving to keep even the rights they formerly had of voting and working and moving as freemen. Schemes of migration and colonization arose among them; but these they refused to entertain, and they eventually turned to the Abolition movement as a final refuge.

Here, led by Remond, Nell, Wells-Brown, and Douglass, a new period of self-assertion and self-development dawned. To be sure, ultimate freedom and assimilation was the ideal before the leaders, but the assertion of the manhood rights of the Negro by himself was the main reliance, and John Brown's raid was the extreme of its logic. After the war and emancipation, the great form of Frederick Douglass, the greatest of American Negro leaders, still led the host. Self-assertion, especially in political lines, was the main programme, and behind Douglass came Elliot, Bruce, and Langston, and the Reconstruction politicians, and, less conspicuous but of greater social significance, Alexander Crummell and Bishop Daniel Payne.

Then came the Revolution of 1876, the suppression of the Negro votes, the changing and shifting of ideals, and the seeking of new lights in the great night. Douglass, in his old age, still bravely stood for the ideals of his early manhood,—ultimate assimilation through self-assertion, and on no other terms. For a time Price arose as a new leader, destined, it seemed, not to give up, but to re-state the old ideals in a form less repugnant to the white South. But he passed away in his prime. Then came the new leader. Nearly all the former ones had become leaders by the silent suffrage of their fellows, had sought to lead their own people alone, and were usually, save Douglass, little known outside their race. But Booker T. Washington arose as essentially the leader not of one race but of two,—a compromiser between the South, the North, and the Negro. Naturally the Negroes resented, at first bitterly, signs of compromise which surrendered their civil and political rights, even though this was to be exchanged for larger chances of economic development. The rich and dominating North, however, was not only weary of the race problem, but was investing largely in Southern enterprises, and welcomed any method of peaceful cooperation. Thus, by national opinion, the Negroes began to recognize Mr. Washington's leadership; and the voice of criticism was hushed.

Mr. Washington represents in Negro thought the old attitude of adjustment and submission; but adjustment at such a peculiar time as to make his programme unique. This is an age of unusual economic development, and Mr. Washington's programme naturally takes an economic cast, becoming a gospel of Work and Money to such an extent as apparently almost completely to overshadow the higher aims of life. Moreover, this is an age when the more advanced races are coming in closer contact with the less developed races, and the race-feeling is therefore intensified; and Mr. Washington's programme practically accepts the alleged inferiority of the Negro races. Again, in our own land, the reaction from the sentiment of war time has given impetus to race-prejudice against Negroes, and Mr. Washington withdraws many of the high demands of Negroes as men and American citizens. In other periods of intensified prejudice all the Negro's tendency to self-assertion has been called forth; at this period a policy of submission is advocated. In the history of nearly all other races and peoples the doctrine preached at such crises has been that manly self-respect is worth more than lands and houses, and that a people who voluntarily surrender such respect, or cease striving for it, are not worth civilizing.

In answer to this, it has been claimed that the Negro can survive only through submission. Mr. Washington distinctly asks that black people give up, at least for the present, three things,—

First, political power,

Second, insistence on civil rights,

Third, higher education of Negro youth,—and concentrate all their energies on industrial education, and accumulation of wealth, and the conciliation of the South. This policy has been courageously and insistently advocated for over fifteen years, and has been triumphant for perhaps ten years. As a result of this tender of the palm-branch, what has been the return? In these years there have occurred:

1. The disfranchisement of the Negro.

2. The legal creation of a distinct status of civil inferiority for the Negro.

3. The steady withdrawal of aid from institutions for the higher training of the Negro.

These movements are not, to be sure, direct results of Mr. Washington's teachings; but his propaganda has, without a shadow of doubt, helped their speedier accomplishment. The question then comes: Is it possible, and probable, that nine millions of men can make effective progress in economic lines if they are deprived of political rights, made a servile caste, and allowed only the most meagre chance for developing their exceptional men? If history and reason give any distinct answer to these questions, it is an emphatic NO. And Mr. Washington thus faces the triple paradox of his career:

1. He is striving nobly to make Negro artisans business men and property-owners; but it is utterly impossible, under modern competitive methods, for workingmen and property-owners to defend their rights and exist without the right of suffrage.

2. He insists on thrift and self-respect, but at the same time counsels a silent submission to civic inferiority such as is bound to sap the manhood of any race in the long run.

3. He advocates common-school and industrial training, and depreciates institutions of higher learning; but neither the Negro common-schools, nor Tuskegee itself, could remain open a day were it not for teachers trained in Negro colleges, or trained by their graduates.

This triple paradox in Mr. Washington's position is the object of criticism by two classes of colored Americans. One class is spiritually descended from Toussaint the Savior, through Gabriel, Vesey, and Turner, and they represent the attitude of revolt and revenge; they hate the white South blindly and distrust the white race generally, and so far as they agree on definite action, think that the Negro's only hope lies in emigration beyond the borders of the United States. And yet, by the irony of fate, nothing has more effectually made this programme seem hopeless than the recent course of the United States toward weaker and darker peoples in the West Indies, Hawaii, and the Philippines,—for where in the world may we go and be safe from lying and brute force?

The other class of Negroes who cannot agree with Mr. Washington has hitherto said little aloud. They deprecate the sight of scattered counsels, of internal disagreement; and especially they dislike making their just criticism of a useful and earnest man an excuse for a general discharge of venom from small-minded opponents. Nevertheless, the questions involved are so fundamental and serious that it is difficult to see how men like the Grimkes, Kelly Miller, J.W.E. Bowen, and other representatives of this group, can much longer be silent. Such men feel in conscience bound to ask of this nation three things:

1. The right to vote.

2. Civic equality.

3. The education of youth according to ability. They acknowledge Mr. Washington's invaluable service in counselling patience and courtesy in such demands; they do not ask that ignorant black men vote when ignorant whites are debarred, or that any reasonable restrictions in the suffrage should not be applied; they know that the low social level of the mass of the race is responsible for much discrimination against it, but they also know, and the nation knows, that relentless color-prejudice is more often a cause than a result of the Negro's degradation; they seek the abatement of this relic of barbarism, and not its systematic encouragement and pampering by all agencies of social power from the Associated Press to the Church of Christ. They advocate, with Mr. Washington, a broad system of Negro common schools supplemented by thorough industrial training; but they are surprised that a man of Mr. Washington's insight cannot see that no such educational system ever has rested or can rest on any other basis than that of the well-equipped college and university, and they insist that there is a demand for a few such institutions throughout the South to train the best of the Negro youth as teachers, professional men, and leaders.

This group of men honor Mr. Washington for his attitude of conciliation toward the white South; they accept the "Atlanta Compromise" in its broadest interpretation; they recognize, with him, many signs of promise, many men of high purpose and fair judgment, in this section; they know that no easy task has been laid upon a region already tottering under heavy burdens. But, nevertheless, they insist that the way to truth and right lies in straightforward honesty, not in indiscriminate flattery; in praising those of the South who do well and criticising uncompromisingly those who do ill; in taking advantage of the opportunities at hand and urging their fellows to do the same, but at the same time in remembering that only a firm adherence to their higher ideals and aspirations will ever keep those ideals within the realm of possibility. They do not expect that the free right to vote, to enjoy civic rights, and to be educated, will come in a moment; they do not expect to see the bias and prejudices of years disappear at the blast of a trumpet; but they are absolutely certain that the way for a people to gain their reasonable rights is not by voluntarily throwing them away and insisting that they do not want them; that the way for a people to gain respect is not by continually belittling and ridiculing themselves; that, on the contrary, Negroes must insist continually, in season and out of season, that voting is necessary to modern manhood, that color discrimination is barbarism, and that black boys need education as well as white boys.

In failing thus to state plainly and unequivocally the legitimate demands of their people, even at the cost of opposing an honored leader, the thinking classes of American Negroes would shirk a heavy responsibility,—a responsibility to themselves, a responsibility to the struggling masses, a responsibility to the darker races of men whose future depends so largely on this American experiment, but especially a responsibility to this nation,—this common Fatherland. It is wrong to encourage a man or a people in evil-doing; it is wrong to aid and abet a national crime simply because it is unpopular not to do so. The growing spirit of kindliness and reconciliation between the North and South after the frightful difference of a generation ago ought to be a source of deep congratulation to all, and especially to those whose mistreatment caused the war; but if that reconciliation is to be marked by the industrial slavery and civic death of those same black men, with permanent legislation into a position of inferiority, then those black men, if they are really men, are called upon by every consideration of patriotism and loyalty to oppose such a course by all civilized methods, even though such opposition involves disagreement with Mr. Booker T. Washington. We have no right to sit silently by while the inevitable seeds are sown for a harvest of disaster to our children, black and white.

First, it is the duty of black men to judge the South discriminatingly. The present generation of Southerners are not responsible for the past, and they should not be blindly hated or blamed for it. Furthermore, to no class is the indiscriminate endorsement of the recent course of the South toward Negroes more nauseating than to the best thought of the South. The South is not "solid"; it is a land in the ferment of social change, wherein forces of all kinds are fighting for supremacy; and to praise the ill the South is today perpetrating is just as wrong as to condemn the good. Discriminating and broad-minded criticism is what the South needs,—needs it for the sake of her own white sons and daughters, and for the insurance of robust, healthy mental and moral development.

Today even the attitude of the Southern whites toward the blacks is not, as so many assume, in all cases the same; the ignorant Southerner hates the Negro, the workingmen fear his competition, the money-makers wish to use him as a laborer, some of the educated see a menace in his upward development, while others—usually the sons of the masters—wish to help him to rise. National opinion has enabled this last class to maintain the Negro common schools, and to protect the Negro partially in property, life, and limb. Through the pressure of the money-makers, the Negro is in danger of being reduced to semi-slavery, especially in the country districts; the workingmen, and those of the educated who fear the Negro, have united to disfranchise him, and some have urged his deportation; while the passions of the ignorant are easily aroused to lynch and abuse any black man. To praise this intricate whirl of thought and prejudice is nonsense; to inveigh indiscriminately against "the South" is unjust; but to use the same breath in praising Governor Aycock, exposing Senator Morgan, arguing with Mr. Thomas Nelson Page, and denouncing Senator Ben Tillman, is not only sane, but the imperative duty of thinking black men.

It would be unjust to Mr. Washington not to acknowledge that in several instances he has opposed movements in the South which were unjust to the Negro; he sent memorials to the Louisiana and Alabama constitutional conventions, he has spoken against lynching, and in other ways has openly or silently set his influence against sinister schemes and unfortunate happenings. Notwithstanding this, it is equally true to assert that on the whole the distinct impression left by Mr. Washington's propaganda is, first, that the South is justified in its present attitude toward the Negro because of the Negro's degradation; secondly, that the prime cause of the Negro's failure to rise more quickly is his wrong education in the past; and, thirdly, that his future rise depends primarily on his own efforts. Each of these propositions is a dangerous half-truth. The supplementary truths must never be lost sight of: first, slavery and race-prejudice are potent if not sufficient causes of the Negro's position; second, industrial and common-school training were necessarily slow in planting because they had to await the black teachers trained by higher institutions,—it being extremely doubtful if any essentially different development was possible, and certainly a Tuskegee was unthinkable before 1880; and, third, while it is a great truth to say that the Negro must strive and strive mightily to help himself, it is equally true that unless his striving be not simply seconded, but rather aroused and encouraged, by the initiative of the richer and wiser environing group, he cannot hope for great success.

In his failure to realize and impress this last point, Mr. Washington is especially to be criticised. His doctrine has tended to make the whites, North and South, shift the burden of the Negro problem to the Negro's shoulders and stand aside as critical and rather pessimistic spectators; when in fact the burden belongs to the nation, and the hands of none of us are clean if we bend not our energies to righting these great wrongs.

The South ought to be led, by candid and honest criticism, to assert her better self and do her full duty to the race she has cruelly wronged and is still wronging. The North—her co-partner in guilt—cannot salve her conscience by plastering it with gold. We cannot settle this problem by diplomacy and suaveness, by "policy" alone. If worse come to worst, can the moral fibre of this country survive the slow throttling and murder of nine millions of men?

The black men of America have a duty to perform, a duty stern and delicate,—a forward movement to oppose a part of the work of their greatest leader. So far as Mr. Washington preaches Thrift, Patience, and Industrial Training for the masses, we must hold up his hands and strive with him, rejoicing in his honors and glorying in the strength of this Joshua called of God and of man to lead the headless host. But so far as Mr. Washington apologizes for injustice, North or South, does not rightly value the privilege and duty of voting, belittles the emasculating effects of caste distinctions, and opposes the higher training and ambition of our brighter minds,—so far as he, the South, or the Nation, does this,—we must unceasingly and firmly oppose them. By every civilized and peaceful method we must strive for the rights which the world accords to men, clinging unwaveringly to those great words which the sons of the Fathers would fain forget: "We hold these truths to be self-evident: That all men are created equal; that they are endowed by their Creator with certain unalienable rights; that among these are life, liberty, and the pursuit of happiness."

OF ALEXANDER CRUMMELL (1903)[18]

Then from the Dawn it seemed there came, but faint
As from beyond the limit of the world,
Like the last echo born of a great cry,
Sounds, as if some fair city were one voice
Around a king returning from his wars.

—TENNYSON

This is the story of a human heart,—the tale of a black boy who many long years ago began to struggle with life that he might know the world and know himself. Three temptations he met on those dark dunes that lay gray and dismal before the wonder-eyes of the child: the temptation of Hate, that stood out against the red dawn; the temptation of Despair, that darkened noonday; and the temptation of Doubt, that ever steals along with twilight. Above all, you must hear of the vales he crossed,—the Valley of Humiliation and the Valley of the Shadow of Death.

I saw Alexander Crummell first at a Wilberforce commencement season, amid its bustle and crush. Tall, frail, and black he stood, with simple dignity and an unmistakable air of good breeding. I talked with him apart, where the storming of the lusty young orators could not harm us. I spoke to him politely, then curiously, then eagerly, as I began to feel the fineness of his character,—his calm courtesy, the sweetness of his strength, and his fair blending of the hope and truth of life. Instinctively I bowed before this man, as one bows before the prophets of the world. Some seer he seemed, that came not from the crimson Past or the gray To-come, but from the pulsing Now,—that mocking world which seemed to

---

18   Originally appeared in *The Souls of Black Folk*, A.C. McClurg & Co. 1903.

me at once so light and dark, so splendid and sordid. Fourscore years had he wandered in this same world of mine, within the Veil.

He was born with the Missouri Compromise and lay a-dying amid the echoes of Manila and El Caney: stirring times for living, times dark to look back upon, darker to look forward to. The black-faced lad that paused over his mud and marbles seventy years ago saw puzzling vistas as he looked down the world. The slave-ship still groaned across the Atlantic, faint cries burdened the Southern breeze, and the great black father whispered mad tales of cruelty into those young ears. From the low doorway the mother silently watched her boy at play, and at nightfall sought him eagerly lest the shadows bear him away to the land of slaves.

So his young mind worked and winced and shaped curiously a vision of Life; and in the midst of that vision ever stood one dark figure alone,—ever with the hard, thick countenance of that bitter father, and a form that fell in vast and shapeless folds. Thus the temptation of Hate grew and shadowed the growing child,—gliding stealthily into his laughter, fading into his play, and seizing his dreams by day and night with rough, rude turbulence. So the black boy asked of sky and sun and flower the never-answered Why? and loved, as he grew, neither the world nor the world's rough ways.

Strange temptation for a child, you may think; and yet in this wide land to-day a thousand thousand dark children brood before this same temptation, and feel its cold and shuddering arms. For them, perhaps, some one will some day lift the Veil,—will come tenderly and cheerily into those sad little lives and brush the brooding hate away, just as Beriah Green strode in upon the life of Alexander Crummell. And before the bluff, kind-hearted man the shadow seemed less dark. Beriah Green had a school in Oneida County, New York, with a score of mischievous boys. "I'm going to bring a black boy here to educate," said Beriah Green, as only a crank and an abolitionist would have dared to say. "Oho!"

laughed the boys. "Ye-es," said his wife; and Alexander came. Once before, the black boy had sought a school, had travelled, cold and hungry, four hundred miles up into free New Hampshire, to Canaan. But the godly farmers hitched ninety yoke of oxen to the abolition schoolhouse and dragged it into the middle of the swamp. The black boy trudged away.

The nineteenth was the first century of human sympathy,—the age when half wonderingly we began to descry in others that transfigured spark of divinity which we call Myself; when clod-hoppers and peasants, and tramps and thieves, and millionaires and—sometimes—Negroes, became throbbing souls whose warm pulsing life touched us so nearly that we half gasped with surprise, crying, "Thou too! Hast Thou seen Sorrow and the dull waters of Hopelessness? Hast Thou known Life?" And then all helplessly we peered into those Other-worlds, and wailed, "O World of Worlds, how shall man make you one?"

So in that little Oneida school there came to those schoolboys a revelation of thought and longing beneath one black skin, of which they had not dreamed before. And to the lonely boy came a new dawn of sympathy and inspiration. The shadowy, formless thing—the temptation of Hate, that hovered between him and the world—grew fainter and less sinister. It did not wholly fade away, but diffused itself and lingered thick at the edges. Through it the child now first saw the blue and gold of life,—the sun-swept road that ran 'twixt heaven and earth until in one far-off wan waver-ing line they met and kissed. A vision of life came to the growing boy,—mystic, wonderful. He raised his head, stretched himself, breathed deep of the fresh new air. Yonder, behind the forests, he heard strange sounds; then glinting through the trees he saw, far, far away, the bronzed hosts of a nation calling,—calling faintly, calling loudly. He heard the hateful clank of their chains; he felt them cringe and grovel, and there rose within him a protest and a prophecy. And he girded himself to walk down the world.

A voice and vision called him to be a priest,—a seer to lead the uncalled out of the house of bondage. He saw the headless host turn toward him like the whirling of mad waters,—he stretched forth his hands eagerly, and then, even as he stretched them, suddenly there swept across the vision the temptation of Despair.

They were not wicked men,—the problem of life is not the problem of the wicked,—they were calm, good men, Bishops of the Apostolic Church of God, and strove toward righteousness. They said slowly, "It is all very natural—it is even commendable; but the General Theological Seminary of the Episcopal Church cannot admit a Negro." And when that thin, half-grotesque figure still haunted their doors, they put their hands kindly, half sorrowfully, on his shoulders, and said, "Now,—of course, we—we know how YOU feel about it; but you see it is impossible,—that is—well—it is premature. Sometime, we trust—sincerely trust—all such distinctions will fade away; but now the world is as it is."

This was the temptation of Despair; and the young man fought it doggedly. Like some grave shadow he flitted by those halls, pleading, arguing, half angrily demanding admittance, until there came the final NO: until men hustled the disturber away, marked him as foolish, unreasonable, and injudicious, a vain rebel against God's law. And then from that Vision Splendid all the glory faded slowly away, and left an earth gray and stern rolling on beneath a dark despair. Even the kind hands that stretched themselves toward him from out the depths of that dull morning seemed but parts of the purple shadows. He saw them coldly, and asked, "Why should I strive by special grace when the way of the world is closed to me?" All gently yet, the hands urged him on,—the hands of young John Jay, that daring father's daring son; the hands of the good folk of Boston, that free city. And yet, with a way to the priesthood of the Church open at last before him, the cloud lingered there; and even when in old St. Paul's the venerable Bishop raised his white arms above the Negro deacon—even then the burden had not lifted from that heart, for there had passed a glory from the earth.

And yet the fire through which Alexander Crummell went did not burn in vain. Slowly and more soberly he took up again his plan of life. More critically he studied the situation. Deep down below the slavery and servitude of the Negro people he saw their fatal weaknesses, which long years of mistreatment had emphasized. The dearth of strong moral character, of unbending righteousness, he felt, was their great shortcoming, and here he would begin. He would gather the best of his people into some little Episcopal chapel and there lead, teach, and inspire them, till the leaven spread, till the children grew, till the world hearkened, till—till—and then across his dream gleamed some faint after-glow of that first fair vision of youth—only an after-glow, for there had passed a glory from the earth.

One day—it was in 1842, and the springtide was struggling merrily with the May winds of New England—he stood at last in his own chapel in Providence, a priest of the Church. The days sped by, and the dark young clergyman labored; he wrote his sermons carefully; he intoned his prayers with a soft, earnest voice; he haunted the streets and accosted the wayfarers; he visited the sick, and knelt beside the dying. He worked and toiled, week by week, day by day, month by month. And yet month by month the congregation dwindled, week by week the hollow walls echoed more sharply, day by day the calls came fewer and fewer, and day by day the third temptation sat clearer and still more clearly within the Veil; a temptation, as it were, bland and smiling, with just a shade of mockery in its smooth tones. First it came casually, in the cadence of a voice: "Oh, colored folks? Yes." Or perhaps more definitely: "What do you EXPECT?" In voice and gesture lay the doubt—the temptation of Doubt. How he hated it, and stormed at it furiously! "Of course they are capable," he cried; "of course they can learn and strive and achieve—" and "Of course," added the temptation softly, "they do nothing of the sort." Of all the three temptations, this one struck the deepest. Hate? He had outgrown so childish a thing. Despair? He had steeled his right arm against it, and fought it with the vigor of determination. But to doubt the worth of his life-work,—to doubt the destiny and capability of the race his soul loved because it was his; to find listless squalor instead of eager endeavor; to hear his own lips whispering, "They do not care; they cannot know; they are dumb driven cattle,—why cast your pearls before swine?"—this, this seemed more than man could bear; and he closed the door, and sank upon the steps of the chancel, and cast his robe upon the floor and writhed.

The evening sunbeams had set the dust to dancing in the gloomy chapel when he arose. He folded his vestments, put away the hymn-books, and closed the great Bible. He stepped out into the twilight, looked back upon the narrow little pulpit with a weary smile, and locked the door. Then he walked briskly to the Bishop, and told the Bishop what the Bishop already knew. "I have failed," he said simply. And gaining courage by the confession, he added: "What I need is a larger constituency. There are comparatively few Negroes here, and perhaps they are not of the best. I must go where the field is wider, and try again." So the Bishop sent him to Philadelphia, with a letter to Bishop Onderdonk.

Bishop Onderdonk lived at the head of six white steps,—corpulent, red-faced, and the author of several thrilling tracts on Apostolic Succession. It was after dinner, and the Bishop had settled himself for a pleasant season of contemplation, when the bell must needs ring, and there must burst in upon the Bishop a letter and a thin, ungainly Negro. Bishop Onderdonk read the letter hastily and frowned. Fortunately, his mind was already clear on this point; and he cleared his brow and looked at Crummell. Then he said, slowly and impressively: "I will receive you into this diocese on one condition: no Negro priest can sit in my church convention, and no Negro church must ask for representation there."

I sometimes fancy I can see that tableau: the frail black figure, nervously twitching his hat before the massive abdomen of Bishop Onderdonk; his threadbare coat thrown against the dark wood-work of the bookcases, where Fox's "Lives of the Martyrs" nestled happily beside "The Whole Duty of Man." I seem to see the wide eyes of the Negro wander past the Bishop's broadcloth to where the swinging glass doors of the cabinet glow in the sunlight. A little blue fly is trying to cross the yawning keyhole. He marches briskly up to it, peers into the chasm in a surprised sort of way, and rubs his feelers reflectively; then he essays its depths, and, finding it bottomless, draws back again. The dark-faced priest finds himself wondering if the fly too has faced its Valley of Humiliation, and if it will plunge into it,—when lo! it spreads its tiny wings and buzzes merrily across, leaving the watcher wingless and alone.

Then the full weight of his burden fell upon him. The rich walls wheeled away, and before him lay the cold rough moor winding on through life, cut in twain by one thick granite ridge,—here, the Valley of Humiliation; yonder, the Valley of the Shadow of Death. And I know not which be darker,—no, not I. But this I know: in yonder Vale of the Humble stand to-day a million swarthy men, who willingly would

> "... bear the whips and scorns of time,
> The oppressor's wrong, the proud man's contumely,
> The pangs of despised love, the law's delay,
> The insolence of office, and the spurns
> That patient merit of the unworthy takes,"—

all this and more would they bear did they but know that this were sacrifice and not a meaner thing. So surged the thought within that lone black breast. The Bishop cleared his throat suggestively; then, recollecting that there was really nothing to say, considerately said nothing, only sat tapping his foot impatiently. But Alexander Crummell said, slowly and heavily: "I will never enter your diocese on such terms." And saying this, he turned and passed into the Valley of the Shadow of Death. You might have noted only the physical dying, the shattered frame and hacking cough; but in that soul lay deeper death than that. He found a chapel in New York,—the church of his father; he labored for it in poverty and starvation, scorned by his fellow priests. Half in despair, he wandered across the sea, a beggar with outstretched hands. Englishmen clasped them,—Wilberforce and Stanley, Thirwell and Ingles, and even Froude and Macaulay; Sir Benjamin Brodie bade him rest awhile at Queen's College in Cambridge, and there he lingered, struggling for health of body and mind, until he took his degree in '53. Restless still, and unsatisfied, he turned toward Africa, and for long years, amid the spawn of the slave-smugglers, sought a new heaven and a new earth.

So the man groped for light; all this was not Life,—it was the world-wandering of a soul in search of itself, the striving of one who vainly sought his place in the world, ever haunted by the shadow of a death that is more than death,—the passing of a soul that has missed its duty. Twenty years he wandered,—twenty years and more; and yet the hard rasping question kept gnawing within him, "What, in God's name, am I on earth for?" In the narrow New York parish his soul seemed cramped and smothered. In the fine old air of the English University he heard the millions wailing over the sea. In the wild fever-cursed swamps of West Africa he stood helpless and alone.

You will not wonder at his weird pilgrimage,—you who in the swift whirl of living, amid its cold paradox and marvellous vision, have fronted life and asked its riddle face to face. And if you find that riddle hard to read, remember that yonder black boy finds it just a little harder; if it is difficult for you to find and face your duty, it is a shade more difficult for him; if your heart sickens in the blood and dust of battle, remember that to him the dust is thicker and the battle fiercer. No wonder the wanderers fall! No wonder we point to thief and murderer, and haunting prostitute, and the never-ending throng of unhearsed dead! The Valley of the Shadow of Death gives few of its pilgrims back to the world.

But Alexander Crummell it gave back. Out of the temptation of Hate, and burned by the fire of Despair, triumphant over Doubt, and steeled by Sacrifice against Humiliation, he turned at last home across the waters, humble and strong, gentle and determined. He bent to all the gibes and prejudices, to all hatred and discrimination, with that rare courtesy which is the armor of pure souls. He fought among his own, the low, the grasping, and the wicked, with that unbending righteousness which is the sword of the just. He never faltered, he seldom complained; he simply worked, inspiring the young, rebuking the old, helping the weak, guiding the strong.

So he grew, and brought within his wide influence all that was best of those who walk within the Veil. They who live without knew not nor dreamed of that full power within, that mighty inspiration which the dull gauze of caste decreed that most men should not know. And now that he is gone, I sweep the Veil away and cry, Lo! the soul to whose dear memory I bring this little tribute. I can see his face still, dark and heavy-lined beneath his snowy hair; lighting and shading, now with inspiration for the future, now in innocent pain at some human wickedness, now with sorrow at some hard memory from the past. The more I met Alexander Crummell, the

73

more I felt how much that world was losing which knew so little of him. In another age he might have sat among the elders of the land in purple-bordered toga; in another country mothers might have sung him to the cradles.

He did his work,—he did it nobly and well; and yet I sorrow that here he worked alone, with so little human sympathy. His name to-day, in this broad land, means little, and comes to fifty million ears laden with no incense of memory or emulation. And herein lies the tragedy of the age: not that men are poor,—all men know something of poverty; not that men are wicked,—who is good? not that men are ignorant,—what is Truth? Nay, but that men know so little of men.

He sat one morning gazing toward the sea. He smiled and said, "The gate is rusty on the hinges." That night at starrise a wind came moaning out of the west to blow the gate ajar, and then the soul I loved fled like a flame across the Seas, and in its seat sat Death.

I wonder where he is to-day? I wonder if in that dim world beyond, as he came gliding in, there rose on some wan throne a King,—a dark and pierced Jew, who knows the writhings of the earthly damned, saying, as he laid those heart-wrung talents down, "Well done!" while round about the morning stars sat singing.

OF THE COMING OF JOHN (1903)[19]

What bring they 'neath the midnight,
Beside the River–sea?
They bring the human heart wherein
No nightly calm can be;
That droppeth never with the wind,
Nor drieth with the dew;
O calm it, God; thy calm is broad
To cover spirits too.

The river floweth on.

—MRS. BROWNING.[20]

C ARLISLE Street runs westward from the centre of Johnstown, across a great black bridge, down a hill and up again, by little shops and meat-markets, past single-storied homes, until suddenly it stops against a wide green lawn. It is a broad, restful place, with two large buildings outlined against the west. When at evening the winds come swelling from the east, and the great pall of the city's smoke hangs wearily above the valley, then the red west glows like a dreamland down Carlisle Street, and, at the tolling of the supper-bell, throws the passing forms of students in dark silhouette against the sky. Tall and black, they move slowly by, and seem in the sinister light to flit before the city like dim warning ghosts. Perhaps they are; for this is Wells Institute, and these black students have few dealings with the white city below.

---

19   Originally appeared in *The Souls of Black Folk*, A.C. McClurg & Co. 1903.
20   From the Elizabeth Barrett Browning poem "A Romance of the Ganges." From Longfellow's *Poems of Places: An Anthology in 31 Volumes.* (1874).

And if you will notice, night after night, there is one dark form that ever hurries last and late toward the twinkling lights of Swain Hall,—for Jones is never on time. A long, straggling fellow he is, brown and hard-haired, who seems to be growing straight out of his clothes, and walks with a half-apologetic roll. He used perpetually to set the quiet dining-room into waves of merriment, as he stole to his place after the bell had tapped for prayers; he seemed so perfectly awkward. And yet one glance at his face made one forgive him much,—that broad, good-natured smile in which lay no bit of art or artifice, but seemed just bubbling good-nature and genuine satisfaction with the world.

He came to us from Altamaha, away down there beneath the gnarled oaks of Southeastern Georgia, where the sea croons to the sands and the sands listen till they sink half drowned beneath the waters, rising only here and there in long, low islands. The white folk of Altamaha voted John a good boy,—fine plough-hand, good in the rice-fields, handy everywhere, and always good-natured and respectful. But they shook their heads when his mother wanted to send him off to school. "It'll spoil him,—ruin him," they said; and they talked as though they knew.

But full half the black folk followed him proudly to the station, and carried his queer little trunk and many bundles. And there they shook and shook hands, and the girls kissed him shyly and the boys clapped him on the back. So the train came, and he pinched his little sister lovingly, and put his great arms about his mother's

Video Sidebar

Westbrook talks about his favorite Du Bois work, the moving story "Of the Coming of John."

http://youtu.be/_3XIsrBVGgw

neck, and then was away with a puff and a roar into the great yellow world that flamed and flared about the doubtful pilgrim. Up the coast they hurried, past the squares and palmettos of Savannah, through the cotton-fields and through the weary night, to Millville, and came with the morning to the noise and bustle of Johnstown.

And they that stood behind, that morning in Altamaha, and watched the train as it noisily bore playmate and brother and son away to the world, had thereafter one ever-recurring word,—"When John comes." Then what parties were to be, and what speakings in the churches; what new furniture in the front room,—perhaps even a new front room; and there would be a new schoolhouse, with John as teacher; and then perhaps a big wedding; all this and more—when John comes. But the white people shook their heads.

At first he was coming at Christmas-time,—but the vacation proved too short; and then, the next summer, but times were hard and schooling costly, and so, instead, he worked in Johnstown.

And so it drifted to the next summer, and the next,—till playmates scattered, and mother grew gray, and sister went up to the Judge's kitchen to work. And still the legend lingered,—"When John comes."

Up at the Judge's they rather liked this refrain; for they too had a John—a fair-haired, smooth-faced boy, who had played many a long summer's day to its close with his darker namesake. "Yes, sir! John is at Princeton, sir," said the broad-shouldered gray-haired Judge every morning as he marched down to the post-office. "Showing the Yankees what a Southern gentleman can do," he added; and strode home again with his letters and papers. Up at the great pillared house they lingered long over the Princeton letter,—the Judge and his frail wife, his sister and growing daughters. "It'll make a man of him," said the Judge, "college is the place." And then he asked the shy little waitress, "Well, Jennie, how's your

John?" and added reflectively, "Too bad, too bad your mother sent him off,—it will spoil him." And the waitress wondered.

Thus in the far-away Southern village the world lay waiting, half consciously, the coming of two young men, and dreamed in an inarticulate way of new things that would be done and new thoughts that all would think. And yet it was singular that few thought of two Johns,—for the black folk thought of one John, and he was black; and the white folk thought of another John, and he was white. And neither world thought the other world's thought, save with a vague unrest.

Up in Johnstown, at the Institute, we were long puzzled at the case of John Jones. For a long time the clay seemed unfit for any sort of moulding. He was loud and boisterous, always laughing and singing, and never able to work consecutively at anything. He did not know how to study; he had no idea of thoroughness; and with his tardiness, carelessness, and appalling good—humor, we were sore perplexed. One night we sat in faculty-meeting, worried and serious; for Jones was in trouble again. This last escapade was too much, and so we solemnly voted "that Jones, on account of repeated disorder and inattention to work, be suspended for the rest of the term."

It seemed to us that the first time life ever struck Jones as a really serious thing was when the Dean told him he must leave school. He stared at the gray-haired man blankly, with great eyes. "Why,—why," he faltered, "but—I haven't graduated!" Then the Dean slowly and clearly explained, reminding him of the tardiness and the carelessness, of the poor lessons and neglected work, of the noise and disorder, until the fellow hung his head in confusion. Then he said quickly, "But you won't tell mammy and sister,—you won't write mammy, now will you? For if you won't I'll go out into the city and work, and come back next term and show you something." So the Dean promised faithfully, and John shouldered his little trunk, giving neither word nor look to the giggling boys, and walked down Carlisle Street to the great city, with sober eyes and a set and serious face.

Perhaps we imagined it, but someway it seemed to us that the serious look that crept over his boyish face that afternoon never left it again. When he came back to us he went to, work with all his rugged strength. It was a hard struggle, for things did not come easily to him,—few crowding memories of early life and teaching came to help him on his new way; but all the world toward which he strove was of his own building, and he builded slow and hard. As the light dawned lingeringly on his new creations, he sat rapt and silent before the vision, or wandered alone over the green campus peering through and beyond the world of men into a world of thought. And the thoughts at times puzzled him sorely; he could not see just why the circle was not square, and carried it out fifty-six decimal places one midnight— would have gone further, indeed, had not the matron rapped for lights out. He caught terrible colds lying on his back in the meadows of nights, trying to think out the solar system; he had grave doubts as to the ethics of the Fall of Rome, and strongly suspected the Germans of being thieves and rascals, despite his text-books; he pondered long over every new Greek word, and wondered why this meant that and why it couldn't mean something else, and how it must have felt to think all things in Greek. So he thought and puzzled along for himself,—pausing perplexed where others skipped merrily, and walking steadily through the difficulties where the rest stopped and surrendered.

Thus he grew in body and soul, and with him his clothes seemed to grow and arrange themselves; coat sleeves got longer, cuffs appeared, and collars got less soiled. Now and then his boots shone, and a new dignity crept into his walk. And we who saw daily a new thoughtfulness growing in his eyes began to expect something of this plodding boy. Thus he passed out of the preparatory school into college, and we who watched him felt four more years of change, which almost transformed the tall, grave man who bowed to us commencement morning. He had left his queer thought-world and come back to a world of motion and of men. He looked now for the first time sharply about him, and wondered he had seen so little before. He grew slowly to feel almost for the first time the Veil that lay between him and the white world; he first noticed now the oppression that had not seemed oppression before, differences that erstwhile seemed natural, restraints and slights that in his boyhood days had gone unnoticed or been greeted with a laugh. He felt angry now when men did not call him "Mister," he clenched his hands at the "Jim Crow" cars, and chafed at the color-line that hemmed in him and his. A tinge of sarcasm crept into his speech, and a vague bitterness into his life; and he sat long hours wondering and planning a way around these crooked things. Daily he found himself shrinking from the choked and narrow life of his native town. And yet he always planned to go back to Altamaha,—always planned to work there. Still, more and more as the day approached he hesitated with a nameless dread; and even the day after graduation he seized with eagerness the offer of the Dean to send him North with the quartette during the summer vacation, to sing for the Institute. A breath of air before the plunge, he said to himself in half apology.

It was a bright September afternoon, and the streets of New York were brilliant with moving men. They reminded John of the sea, as he sat in the square and watched them, so changelessly changing, so bright and dark, so grave and gay. He scanned their rich and faultless clothes, the way they carried their hands, the shape of their hats; he peered into the hurrying carriages. Then, leaning back with a sigh, he said, "This is the World." The notion suddenly seized him to see where the world was going; since many of the richer and brighter seemed hurrying all one way. So when a tall, light-haired young man and a little talkative lady came by, he rose half hesitatingly and followed them. Up the street they went, past stores and gay shops, across a broad square, until with a hundred others they entered the high portal of a great building.

He was pushed toward the ticket office with the others, and felt in his pocket for the new five-dollar bill he had hoarded. There seemed really no time for hesitation, so he drew it bravely out, passed it to the busy clerk, and received simply a ticket but no change. When at last he realized that he had paid five dollars to enter he knew not what, he stood stock-still amazed. "Be careful," said a low voice behind him; "you must not lynch the colored-gentleman simply because he's in your way," and a girl looked up roguishly into the eyes of her fair-haired escort. A shade of annoyance passed over the escort's face. "You WILL not under-stand us at the South," he said half impatiently, as if continuing an argument. "With all your professions, one never sees in the North so cordial and intimate relations between white and black as are everyday occurrences with us. Why, I remember my clos-est playfellow in boyhood was a little Negro named after me, and surely no two,—WELL!" The man stopped short and flushed to the roots of his hair, for there directly beside his reserved orches-tra chairs sat the Negro he had stumbled over in the hallway. He hesitated and grew pale with anger, called the usher and gave him his card, with a few peremptory words, and slowly sat down. The lady deftly changed the subject.

All this John did not see, for he sat in a half-maze minding the scene about him; the delicate beauty of the hall, the faint perfume, the moving myriad of men, the rich clothing and low hum of talking seemed all a part of a world so different from his, so strangely more beautiful than anything he had known, that he sat in dreamland, and started when, after a hush, rose high and clear the music of Lohengrin's swan. The infinite beauty of the wail lingered and swept through every muscle of his frame, and put it all a-tune. He closed his eyes and grasped the elbows of the chair, touching unwittingly the lady's arm. And the lady drew away. A deep longing swelled in all his heart to rise with that clear music out of the dirt and dust of that low life that held him prisoned and befouled. If he could only live up in the free air where birds sang and setting suns had no touch of blood! Who had called him to be the slave and butt of all? And if he had called, what right had he to call when a world like this lay open before men?

Then the movement changed, and fuller, mightier harmony swelled away. He looked thoughtfully across the hall, and wondered why the beautiful gray-haired woman looked so listless, and what the little man could be whispering about. He would not like to be listless and idle, he thought, for he felt with the music the movement of power within him. If he but had some master-work, some life-service, hard,—aye, bitter hard, but without the cringing and sickening servility, without the cruel hurt that hardened his heart and soul. When at last a soft sorrow crept across the violins, there came to him the vision of a far-off home, the great eyes of his sister, and the dark drawn face of his mother. And his heart sank below the waters, even as the sea-sand sinks by the shores of Altamaha, only to be lifted aloft again with that last ethereal wail of the swan that quivered and faded away into the sky.

It left John sitting so silent and rapt that he did not for some time notice the usher tapping him lightly on the shoulder and saying politely, "Will you step this way, please, sir?" A little surprised, he arose quickly at the last tap, and, turning to leave his seat, looked full into the face of the fair-haired young man. For the first time the young man recognized his dark boyhood playmate, and John knew that it was the Judge's son. The white John started, lifted his hand, and then froze into his chair; the black John smiled lightly, then grimly, and followed the usher down the aisle. The manager was sorry, very, very sorry,—but he explained that some mistake had been made in selling the gentleman a seat already disposed of; he would refund the money, of course,—and indeed felt the matter keenly, and so forth, and—before he had finished John was gone, walking hurriedly across the square and down the broad streets, and as he passed the park he buttoned his coat and said, "John Jones, you're a natural-born fool." Then he went to his lodgings and wrote a letter, and tore it up; he wrote another, and threw it in the fire. Then he seized a scrap of paper and wrote: "Dear Mother and Sister—I am coming—John."

"Perhaps," said John, as he settled himself on the train, "perhaps I am to blame myself in struggling against my manifest destiny simply because it looks hard and unpleasant. Here is my duty to Altamaha plain before me; perhaps they'll let me help settle the Negro problems there,—perhaps they won't. "I will go in to the King, which is not according to the law; and if I perish, I perish." And then he mused and dreamed, and planned a life-work; and the train flew south.

Down in Altamaha, after seven long years, all the world knew John was coming. The homes were scrubbed and scoured,—above all, one; the gardens and yards had an unwonted trimness, and Jennie bought a new gingham. With some finesse and negotiation, all the dark Methodists and Presbyterians were induced to join in a monster welcome at the Baptist Church; and as the day drew near, warm discussions arose on every comer as to the exact extent and nature of John's accomplishments. It was noontide on a gray and cloudy day when he came. The black town flocked to the depot, with a little of the white at the edges,—a happy throng, with "Good-mawnings" and "Howdys" and laughing and joking and jostling. Mother sat yonder in the window watching; but sister Jennie stood on the platform, nervously fingering her dress,—tall and lithe, with soft brown skin and loving eyes peering from out a tangled wilderness of hair.

John rose gloomily as the train stopped, for he was thinking of the "Jim Crow" car; he stepped to the platform, and paused: a little dingy station, a black crowd gaudy and dirty, a half-mile of dilapidated shanties along a straggling ditch of mud. An overwhelming sense of the sordidness and narrowness of it all seized him; he looked in vain for his mother, kissed coldly the tall, strange girl who called him brother, spoke a short, dry word here and there; then, lingering neither for hand-shaking nor gossip, started silently up the street, raising his hat merely to the last eager old aunty, to her open-mouthed astonishment. The people were distinctly bewildered. This silent, cold man,—was this John? Where was his smile and hearty hand-grasp? "Peared kind o' down in the mouf," said the Methodist preacher thoughtfully. "Seemed monstus stuck up," complained a Baptist sister. But the white postmaster from the edge of the crowd expressed the opinion of his folks plainly. "That damn Nigger," said he, as he shouldered the mail and arranged his tobacco, "has gone North and got plum full o' fool notions; but they won't work in Altamaha." And the crowd melted away.

The meeting of welcome at the Baptist Church was a failure. Rain spoiled the barbecue; and thunder turned the milk in the ice-cream. When the speaking came at night, the house was crowded to overflowing. The three preachers had especially prepared themselves, but somehow John's manner seemed to throw a blanket over everything,—he seemed so cold and preoccupied, and had so strange an air of restraint that the Methodist brother could not warm up to his theme and elicited not a single "Amen"; the Presbyterian prayer was but feebly responded to, and even the Baptist preacher, though he wakened faint enthusiasm, got so mixed up in his favorite sentence that he had to close it by stopping

84

fully fifteen minutes sooner than he meant. The people moved uneasily in their seats as John rose to reply. He spoke slowly and methodically. The age, he said, demanded new ideas; we were far different from those men of the seventeenth and eighteenth centuries,—with broader ideas of human brotherhood and destiny. Then he spoke of the rise of charity and popular education, and particularly of the spread of wealth and work.

The question was, then, he added reflectively, looking at the low discolored ceiling, what part the Negroes of this land would take in the striving of the new century. He sketched in vague outline the new Industrial School that might rise among these pines, he spoke in detail of the charitable and philanthropic work that might be organized, of money that might be saved for banks and business. Finally he urged unity, and deprecated especially religious and denominational bickering. "To-day," he said, with a smile, "the world cares little whether a man be Baptist or Methodist, or indeed a churchman at all, so long as he is good and true. What difference does it make whether a man be baptized in river or wash-bowl, or not at all? Let's leave all that littleness, and look higher." Then, thinking of nothing else, he slowly sat down. A painful hush seized that crowded mass. Little had they understood of what he said, for he spoke an unknown tongue, save the last word about baptism; that they knew, and they sat very still while the clock ticked. Then at last a low suppressed snarl came from the Amen comer, and an old bent man arose, walked over the seats, and climbed straight up into the pulpit. He was wrinkled and black, with scant gray and tufted hair; his voice and hands shook as with palsy; but on his face lay the intense rapt look of the religious fanatic. He seized the Bible with his rough, huge hands; twice he raised it inarticulate, and then fairly burst into the words, with rude and awful eloquence. He quivered, swayed, and bent; then rose aloft in perfect majesty, till the people moaned and wept, wailed and shouted, and a wild shrieking arose from the comers where all the pent-up feeling of the hour gathered itself and rushed into the air. John never knew clearly what the old man said; he only felt himself held up to scorn and scathing denunciation for trampling on the true Religion, and he realized with amazement that all unknowingly he had put rough, rude hands on something this little world held sacred. He arose silently, and passed out into the night. Down toward the sea he went, in the fitful starlight, half conscious of the girl who followed timidly after him. When at last he stood upon the bluff, he turned to his little sister and looked upon her sorrowfully, remembering with sudden pain how little thought he had given her. He put his arm about her and let her passion of tears spend itself on his shoulder.

Long they stood together, peering over the gray un-resting water.

"John," she said, "does it make everyone —unhappy when they study and learn lots of things?"

He paused and smiled. "I am afraid it does," he said.

"And, John, are you glad you studied?"

"Yes," came the answer, slowly but positively.

She watched the flickering lights upon the sea, and said thoughtfully, "I wish I was unhappy,—and—and," putting both arms about his neck, "I think I am, a little, John."

It was several days later that John walked up to the Judge's house to ask for the privilege of teaching the Negro school. The Judge himself met him at the front door, stared a little hard at him, and said brusquely, "Go 'round to the kitchen door, John, and wait." Sitting on the kitchen steps, John stared at the corn, thoroughly perplexed. What on earth had come over him? Every step he made offended some one. He had come to save his people, and before he left the depot he had hurt them. He sought to teach them at the church, and had outraged their deepest feelings. He had schooled himself to be respectful to the Judge, and then blundered into his front door. And all the time he had meant right,—and yet, and yet, somehow he found it so hard and strange to fit his old surroundings again, to find his place in the world about him. He could not remember that he used to have any difficulty in the past, when life was glad and gay. The world seemed smooth and easy then. Perhaps,—but his sister came to the kitchen door just then and said the Judge awaited him.

The Judge sat in the dining-room amid his morning's mail, and he did not ask John to sit down. He plunged squarely into the business. "You've come for the school, I suppose. Well, John, I want to speak to you plainly. You know I'm a friend to your people. I've helped you and your family, and would have done more if you hadn't got the notion of going off. Now I like the colored people, and sympathize with all their reasonable aspirations; but you and I both know, John, that in this country the Negro must remain subordinate, and can never expect to be the equal of white men. In their place, your people can be honest and respectful; and God knows, I'll do what I can to help them. But when they want to reverse nature, and rule white men, and marry white women, and sit in my parlor, then, by God! We'll hold them under if we have to lynch every Nigger in the land. Now, John, the question is, are you, with your education and Northern notions, going to accept the situation and teach the darkies to be faithful servants and laborers as your fathers were,—I knew your father, John, he belonged to my brother, and he was a good Nigger. Well—well, are you going to be like him, or are you going to try to put fool ideas of rising and equality into these folks' heads, and make them discontented and unhappy?"

"I am going to accept the situation, Judge Henderson," answered John, with a brevity that did not escape the keen old man. He hesitated a moment, and then said shortly, "Very well,—we'll try you awhile. Good-morning."

87

It was a full month after the opening of the Negro school that the other John came home, tall, gay, and headstrong. The mother wept, the sisters sang. The whole white town was glad. A proud man was the Judge, and it was a goodly sight to see the two swinging down Main Street together.

And yet all did not go smoothly between them, for the younger man could not and did not veil his contempt for the little town, and plainly had his heart set on New York. Now the one cherished ambition of the Judge was to see his son mayor of Altamaha, representative to the legislature, and—who could say? —Governor of Georgia. So the argument often waxed hot between them. "Good heavens, father," the younger man would say after dinner, as he lighted a cigar and stood by the fireplace, "you surely don't expect a young fellow like me to settle down permanently in this—this God-forgotten town with nothing but mud and Negroes?" "I did," the Judge would answer laconically; and on this particular day it seemed from the gathering scowl that he was about to add something more emphatic, but neighbors had already begun to drop in to admire his son, and the conversation drifted.

"Heah that John is livenin' things up at the darky school," volunteered the postmaster, after a pause.

"What now?" asked the Judge, sharply.

"Oh, nothin' in particulah,—just his almighty air and uppish ways. B'lieve I did heah somethin' about his givin' talks on the French Revolution, equality, and such like. He's what I call a dangerous Nigger."

"Have you heard him say anything out of the way?"

"Why, no,—but Sally, our girl, told my wife a lot of rot. Then, too, I don't need to heah: a Nigger what won't say 'sir' to a white man, or—"

"Who is this John?" interrupted the son.

"Why, it's little black John, Peggy's son,—your old playfellow."

The young man's face flushed angrily, and then he laughed.

"Oh," said he, "it's the darky that tried to force himself into a seat beside the lady I was escorting—"

But Judge Henderson waited to hear no more. He had been nettled all day, and now at this he rose with a half-smothered oath, took his hat and cane, and walked straight to the schoolhouse.

For John, it had been a long, hard pull to get things started in the rickety old shanty that sheltered his school. The Negroes were rent into factions for and against him, the parents were careless, the children irregular and dirty, and books, pencils, and slates largely missing. Nevertheless, he struggled hopefully on, and seemed to see at last some glimmering of dawn. The attendance was larger and the children were a shade cleaner this week. Even the booby class in reading showed a little comforting progress. So John settled himself with renewed patience this afternoon.

"Now, Mandy," he said cheerfully, "that's better; but you mustn't chop your words up so: 'If—the man—goes.' Why, your little brother even wouldn't tell a story that way, now would he?"

"Naw, suh, he cain't talk"

"All right; now let's try again: 'If the man—'"

"John!"

The whole school started in surprise, and the teacher half arose, as the red, angry face of the Judge appeared in the open doorway.

"John, this school is closed. You children can go home and get to work. The white people of Altamaha are not spending their money on black folks to have their heads crammed with impudence and lies. Clear out! I'll lock the door myself."

Up at the great pillared house the tall young son wandered aimlessly about after his father's abrupt departure. In the house there was little to interest him; the books were old and stale, the local newspaper flat, and the women had retired with headaches and sewing. He tried a nap, but it was too warm. So he sauntered out into the fields, complaining disconsolately, "Good Lord! how long will this imprisonment last!" He was not a bad fellow,—just a little spoiled and self-indulgent, and as headstrong as his proud father. He seemed a young man pleasant to look upon, as he sat on the great black stump at the edge of the pines idly swinging his legs and smoking. "Why, there isn't even a girl worth getting up a respectable flirtation with," he growled. Just then his eye caught a tall, willowy figure hurrying toward him on the narrow path. He looked with interest at first, and then burst into a laugh as he said, "Well, I declare, if it isn't Jennie, the little brown kitchen-maid! Why, I never noticed before what a trim little body she is. Hello, Jennie! Why, you haven't kissed me since I came home," he said gaily. The young girl stared at him in surprise and confusion,—faltered something inarticulate, and attempted to pass. But a willful mood had seized the young idler, and he caught at her arm. Frightened, she slipped by; and half mischievously he turned and ran after her through the tall pines.

The great brown sea lay silent. The air scarce breathed. The dying day bathed the twisted oaks and mighty pines in black and gold. There came from the wind no warning, not a whisper from the cloudless sky. There was only a black man hurrying on with an ache in his heart, seeing neither sun nor sea, but starting as from a dream at the frightened cry that woke the pines, to see his dark sister struggling in the arms of a tall and fair-haired man.

He said not a word, but, seizing a fallen limb, struck him with all the pent-up hatred of his great black arm; and the body lay white and still beneath the pines, all bathed in sunshine and in blood. John looked at it dreamily, then walked back to the house briskly, and said in a soft voice, "Mammy, I'm going away,—I'm going to be free."

She gazed at him dimly and faltered, "No'th, honey, is yo' gwine No'th agin?"

He looked out where the North Star glistened pale above the waters, and said, "Yes, mammy, I'm going—North."

Then, without another word, he went out into the narrow lane, up by the straight pines, to the same winding path, and seated himself on the great black stump, looking at the blood where the body had lain. Yonder in the gray past he had played with that dead boy, romping together under the solemn trees. The night deepened; he thought of the boys at Johnstown. He wondered how Brown had turned out, and Carey? And Jones,—Jones? Why, he was Jones, and he wondered what they would all say when they knew, when they knew, in that great long dining-room with its hundreds of merry eyes. Then as the sheen of the starlight stole over him, he thought of the gilded ceiling of that vast concert hall, and heard stealing toward him the faint sweet music of the swan. Hark! was it music, or the hurry and shouting of men? Yes, surely! Clear and high the faint sweet melody rose and fluttered like a living thing, so that the very earth trembled as with the tramp of horses and murmur of angry men.

He leaned back and smiled toward the sea, whence rose the strange melody, away from the dark shadows where lay the noise of horses galloping, galloping on. With an effort he roused himself, bent forward, and looked steadily down the pathway, softly humming the "Song of the Bride,"—

"Freudig gefiihrt, ziehet dahin." [21]

Amid the trees in the dim morning twilight he watched their shadows dancing and heard their horses thundering toward him, until at last they came sweeping like a storm, and he saw in front that haggard white-haired man, whose eyes flashed red with fury. Oh, how he pitied him,—pitied him,—and wondered if he had

---

21   Translation: "Joyfully guided, come to this place." From Lohengrin's "Song of the Bride" (The song is often referred to as "Here Comes the Bride").

the coiling twisted rope. Then, as the storm burst round him, he rose slowly to his feet and turned his closed eyes toward the Sea. And the world whistled in his ears.

THE TALENTED TENTH (1903)[22]

The Negro race, like all races, is going to be saved by its exceptional men. The problem of education, then, among Negroes must first of all deal with the Talented Tenth; it is the problem of developing the Best of this race that they may guide the Mass away from the contamination and death of the Worst, in their own and other races. Now the training of men is a difficult and intricate task. Its technique is a matter for educational experts, but its object is for the vision of seers. If we make money the object of man-training, we shall develop money-makers but not necessarily men; if we make technical skill the object of education, we may possess artisans but not, in nature, men. Men we shall have only as we make manhood the object of the work of the schools—intelligence, broad sympathy, knowledge of the world that was and is, and of the relation of men to it—this is the curriculum of that Higher Education which must underlie true life. On this foundation we may build bread winning, skill of hand and quickness of brain, with never a fear lest the child and man mistake the means of living for the object of life. If this be true—and who can deny it—three tasks lay before me; first to show from the past that the Talented Tenth as they have risen among American Negroes have been worthy of leadership; secondly to show how these men may be educated and developed; and thirdly to show their relation to the Negro problem.

---

22 Originally appeared in the book, *The Negro Problem: A Series of Articles by Representative Negroes of To-day*, published by J. Pott, New York, 1903.

You misjudge us because you do not know us. From the very first it has been the educated and intelligent of the Negro people that have led and elevated the mass, and the sole obstacles that nullified and retarded their efforts were slavery and race prejudice; for what is slavery but the legalized survival of the unfit and the nullification of the work of natural internal leadership? Negro leadership therefore sought from the first to rid the race of this awful incubus that it might make way for natural selection and the survival of the fittest. In colonial days came Phillis Wheatley and Paul Cuffe striving against the bars of prejudice; and Benjamin Banneker, the almanac maker, voiced their longings when he said to Thomas Jefferson, "I freely and cheerfully acknowledge that I am of the African race and in colour which is natural to them, of the deepest dye; and it is under a sense of the most profound gratitude to the Supreme Ruler of the Universe, that I now confess to you that I am not under that state of tyrannical thraldom and inhuman captivity to which too many of my brethren are doomed, but that I have abundantly tasted of the fruition of those blessings which proceed from that free and unequalled liberty with which you are favored, and which I hope you will willingly allow, you have mercifully received from the immediate hand of that Being from whom proceedeth every good and perfect gift.

"Suffer me to recall to your mind that time, in which the arms of the British crown were exerted with every powerful effort, in order to reduce you to a state of servitude; look back, I entreat

· · · · · · · · · · · · · · · · · **Video** Sidebar · · · · · · · · · · · · · · ·

Westbrook explains Du Bois' favorite work, "The Talented Tenth" and his struggle with the concept that a talented 10th must mean an untalented 90th.

http://youtu.be/wollGiMRCIE

· ·

you, on the variety of dangers to which you were exposed; reflect
on that period in which every human aid appeared unavailable,
and in which even hope and fortitude wore the aspect of inability
to the conflict, and you cannot but be led to a serious and grateful sense of your miraculous and providential preservation, you
cannot but acknowledge, that the present freedom and tranquility
which you enjoy, you have mercifully received, and that a peculiar
blessing of heaven.

"This, sir, was a time when you clearly saw into the injustice of
a state of Slavery, and in which you had just apprehensions of the
horrors of its condition. It was then that your abhorrence thereof
was so excited, that you publicly held forth this true and invaluable doctrine, which is worthy to be recorded and remembered
in all succeeding ages: "We hold these truths to be self evident,
that all men are created equal; that they are endowed with certain
inalienable rights, and that among these are life, liberty and the
pursuit of happiness."

Then came Dr. James Derham, who could tell even the learned
Dr. Rush something of medicine, and Lemuel Haynes, to whom
Middlebury College gave an honorary A.M. in 1804. These and
others we may call the Revolutionary group of distinguished
Negroes—they were persons of marked ability, leaders of a
Talented Tenth, standing conspicuously among the best of their
time. They strove by word and deed to save the color line from
becoming the line between the bond and free, but all they could
do was nullified by Eli Whitney and the Curse of Gold. So they
passed into forgetfulness.

But their spirit did not wholly die; here and there in the early
part of the century came other exceptional men. Some were natural sons of unnatural fathers and were given often a liberal training and thus a race of educated mulattoes sprang up to plead for
black men's rights. There was Ira Aldridge, whom all Europe loved

to honor; there was that Voice crying in the Wilderness, David Walker, and saying:

"I declare it does appear to me as though some nations think God is asleep, or that he made the Africans for nothing else but to dig their mines and work their farms, or they cannot believe history sacred or profane. I ask every man who has a heart, and is blessed with the privilege of believing—Is not God a God of justice to all his creatures? Do you say he is? Then if he gives peace and tranquility to tyrants and permits them to keep our fathers, our mothers, ourselves and our children in eternal ignorance and wretchedness to support them and their families, would he be to us a God of Justice? I ask, O, ye Christians, who hold us and our children in the most abject ignorance and degradation that ever a people were afflicted with since the world began—I say if God gives you peace and tranquility, and suffers you thus to go on afflicting us, and our children, who have never given you the least provocation—would He be to us a God of Justice? If you will allow that we are men, who feel for each other, does not the blood of our fathers and of us, their children, cry aloud to the Lord of Sabaoth against you for the cruelties and murders with which you have and do continue to afflict us?"

This was the wild voice that first aroused Southern legislators in 1829 to the terrors of abolitionism.

In 1831 there met that first Negro convention in Philadelphia, at which the world gaped curiously but which bravely attacked the problems of race and slavery, crying out against persecution and declaring that "Laws as cruel in themselves as they were unconstitutional and unjust, have in many places been enacted against our poor, unfriended and unoffending brethren (without a shadow of provocation on our part), at whose bare recital the very savage draws himself up for fear of contagion—looks noble and prides himself because he bears not the name of Christian."

Side by side this free Negro movement, and the movement for abolition, strove until they merged in to one strong stream. Too little notice has been taken of the work which the Talented Tenth among Negroes took in the great abolition crusade. From the very day that a Philadelphia colored man became the first subscriber to Garrison's "Liberator," to the day when Negro soldiers made the Emancipation Proclamation possible, black leaders worked shoulder to shoulder with white men in a movement, the success of which would have been impossible without them. There was Purvis and Remond, Pennington and Highland Garnett, Sojourner Truth and Alexander Crummell, and above, Frederick Douglass—what would the abolition movement have been without them? They stood as living examples of the possibilities of the Negro race, their own hard experiences and well wrought culture said silently more than all the drawn periods of orators—they were the men who made American slavery impossible. As Maria Weston Chapman said, from the school of anti-slavery agitation, "a throng of authors, editors, lawyers, orators and accomplished gentlemen of color have taken their degree! It has equally implanted hopes and aspirations, noble thoughts, and sublime purposes, in the hearts of both races. It has prepared the white man for the freedom of the black man, and it has made the black man scorn the thought of enslavement, as does a white man, as far as its influence has extended. Strengthen that noble influence! Before its organization, the country only saw here and there in slavery some faithful Cudjoe or Dinah, whose strong natures blossomed even in bondage, like a fine plant beneath a heavy stone. Now, under the elevating and cherishing influence of the American Anti-slavery Society, the colored race, like the white, furnishes Corinthian capitals for the noblest temples."

Where were these black abolitionists trained? Some, like Frederick Douglass, were self-trained, but yet trained liberally;

others, like Alexander Crummell and McCune Smith, graduated from famous foreign universities. Most of them rose up through the colored schools of New York and Philadelphia and Boston, taught by college-bred men like Russworm, of Dartmouth, and college-bred white men like Neveau and Benezet.

After emancipation came a new group of educated and gifted leaders: Langston, Bruce and Elliot, Greener, Williams and Payne. Through political organization, historical and polemic writing and moral regeneration, these men strove to uplift their people. It is the fashion of to-day to sneer at them and to say that with freedom Negro leadership should have begun at the plow and not in the Senate—a foolish and mischievous lie; two hundred and fifty years that black serf toiled at the plow and yet that toiling was in vain till the Senate passed the war amendments; and two hundred and fifty years more the half-free serf of to-day may toil at his plow, but unless he have political rights and righteously guarded civic status, he will still remain the poverty-stricken and ignorant plaything of rascals, that he now is. This all sane men know even if they dare not say it.

And so we come to the present—a day of cowardice and vacillation, of strident wide-voiced wrong and faint hearted compromise; of double-faced dallying with Truth and Right. Who are to-day guiding the work of the Negro people? The "exceptions" of course. And yet so sure as this Talented Tenth is pointed out, the blind worshippers of the Average cry out in alarm: "These are exceptions, look here at death, disease and crime—these are the happy rule." Of course they are the rule, because a silly nation made them the rule: Because for three long centuries this people lynched Negroes who dared to be brave, raped black women who dared to be virtuous, crushed dark-hued youth who dared to be ambitious, and encouraged and made to flourish servility and lewdness and apathy. But nor even this was able to crush all manhood and chastity and aspiration from black folk. A saving remnant continually survives and persists, continually aspires, continually shows itself in thrift and ability and character. Exceptional it is to be sure, but this is its chiefest promise; it shows the capability of Negro blood, the promise of black men. Do Americans ever stop to reflect that there are in this land a million men of Negro blood, well-educated, owners of homes, against the honor of whose womanhood no breath was ever raised, whose men occupy positions of trust and usefulness, and who, judged by any standard, have reached the full measure of the best type of modern European culture? Is it fair, is it decent, is it Christian to ignore these facts of the Negro problem, to belittle such aspiration, to nullify such leadership and seek to crush these people back into the mass out of which by toil and travail, they and their fathers have raised themselves?

Can the masses of the Negro people be in any possible way more quickly raised than by the effort and example of this aristocracy of talent and character? Was there ever a nation on God's fair earth civilized from the bottom upward? Never; it is, ever was and ever will be from the top downward that culture filters. The Talented Tenth rises and pulls all that are worth the saving up to their vantage ground. This is the history of human progress; and the two historic mistakes which have hindered that progress were the thinking first that no more could ever rise save the few already risen; or second, that it would better the uprisen to pull the risen down.

How then shall the leaders of a struggling people be trained and the hands of the risen few strengthened? There can be but one answer: The best and most capable of their youth must be schooled in the colleges and universities of the land. We will not quarrel as to just what the university of the Negro should teach or how it should teach it—I willingly admit that each soul and each race-soul needs its own peculiar curriculum. But this is true: A university is a human invention for the transmission of knowledge and culture from generation to generation, through the training of quick minds and pure hearts, and for this work no other human invention will suffice, not even trade and industrial schools.

All men cannot go to college but some men must; every isolated group or nation must have its yeast, must have for the talented few centers of training where men are not so mystified and befuddled by the hard and necessary toil of earning a living, as to have no aims higher than their bellies, and no God greater than Gold. This is true training, and thus in the beginning were the favored sons of the freedmen trained. Out of the colleges of the North came, after the blood of war, Ware, Cravath, Chase, Andrews, Bumstead and Spence to build the foundations of knowledge and civilization in the black South. Where ought they to have begun to build? At the bottom, of course, quibbles the mole with his eyes in the earth. Aye! truly at the bottom, at the very bottom; at the bottom of knowledge, down in the very depths of knowledge there where the roots of justice strike into the lowest soil of Truth. And so they did begin; they founded colleges, and up from the colleges shot normal schools, and out from the normal schools went teachers, and around the normal teachers clustered other teachers to teach the public schools; the college trained in Greek and Latin and mathematics, 2,000 men; and these men trained full 50,000 others in morals and manners, and they in turn taught thrift and the alphabet to nine millions of men, who to-day hold $300,000,000 of property. It was a miracle—the most wonderful peace-battle of the 19th century, and yet to-day men smile at it, and in fine superiority tell us that it was all a strange mistake; that a proper way to found a system of education is first to gather the children and buy them spelling books and hoes; afterward men may look about for teachers, if haply they may find them; or again they would teach men Work, but as for Life—why, what has Work to do with Life, they ask vacantly.

Was the work of these college founders successful; did it stand the test of time? Did the college graduates, with all their fine theories of life, really live? Are they useful men helping to civilize and elevate their less fortunate fellows? Let us see. Omitting all institutions which have not actually graduated students from a college course, there are to-day in the United States thirty-four institutions giving something above high school training to Negroes and designed especially for this race.

Three of these were established in border States before the War; thirteen were planted by the Freedmen's Bureau in the years 1864–1869; nine were established between 1870 and 1880 by various church bodies; five were established after 1881 by Negro churches, and four are state institutions supported by United States' agricultural funds. In most cases the college departments are small adjuncts to high and common schoolwork. As a matter of fact six institutions—Atlanta, Fisk, Howard, Shaw, Wilberforce and Leland, are the important Negro colleges so far as actual work and number of students are concerned. In all these institutions, seven hundred and fifty Negro college students are enrolled. In grade the best of these colleges are about a year behind the smaller New England colleges and a typical curriculum is that of Atlanta University. Here students from the grammar grades, after a three years' high school course, take a college course of 136 weeks. One-fourth of this time is given to Latin and Greek; one-fifth, to English and modern languages; one-sixth, to history and social science; one-seventh, to natural science; one-eighth to mathematics, and one-eighth to philosophy and pedagogy.

In addition to these students in the South, Negroes have attended Northern colleges for many years. As early as 1826 one was graduated from Bowdoin College, and from that time till to-day nearly every year has seen elsewhere, other such graduates. They have, of course, met much color prejudice. Fifty years ago very few colleges would admit them at all. Even to-day no Negro has ever been admitted to Princeton, and at some other leading institutions they are rather endured than encouraged. Oberlin was the great pioneer in tile work of blotting out the color line in colleges, and has more Negro graduates by far than any other Northern college.

The total number of Negro college graduates up to 1899, (several of the graduates of that year not being reported), was as follows:

	Negro Colleges	White Colleges
Before [18]'76	137	75
'75-80	143	22
'80-85	250	31
'85–90	413	43
'90-95	465	66
'95-99	475	88
Class Unknown	57	64
TOTAL	1,940	389

Of these graduates 2,079 were men and 252 were women; 50 percent of Northern-born college men come South to work among the masses of their people, at a sacrifice which few people realize; nearly 90 per cent of the Southern-born graduates instead of seeking that personal freedom and broader intellectual atmosphere which their training has led them, in some degree, to conceive, stay and labor and wait in the midst of their black neighbors and relatives.

The most interesting question, and in many respects the crucial question, to be asked concerning college-bred Negroes, is: Do they earn a living? It has been intimated more than once that the higher training of Negroes has resulted in sending into the world of work, men who could find nothing to do suitable to their talents. Now and then there comes a rumor of a colored college man working at menial service, etc. Fortunately, returns as to occupations of college-bred Negroes, gathered by the Atlanta conference, are quite full—nearly sixty per cent of the total number of graduates.

This enables us to reach fairly certain conclusions as to the occupations of all college-bred Negroes. Of 1,312 persons reported, there were:

Teachers,	53.4%
Clergymen,	16.8%
Physicians, etc.,	6.3%
Students,	5.6%
Lawyers,	4.7%
In Govt. Service,	4.0%
In Business,	3.6%
Farmers and Artisans,	2.7%
Editors, Secretaries and Clerks,	2.4%
Miscellaneous,	.5%

Over half are teachers, a sixth are preachers, another sixth are students and professional men; over 6 per cent are farmers, artisans and merchants, and 4 per cent are in government service. In detail the occupations are as follows

Occupations of College-Bred Men

Teachers
Presidents and Deans	19	
Teachers of Music	7	
Professors, Principals and Teachers	675	Total 701

Clergymen
Bishop	1

Chaplains, U.S. Army	2	
Missionaries	9	
Predsiding Elders	12	
Preachers	197	Total 221
Physicians:		
Doctors of Medicine,	76	
Druggists,	4	
Dentists,	3	Total 83
Students,		74
Lawyers,		62
Civil Service		
U.S. Minister Plenipotentiary,	1	
U.S. Consul	1	
U.S. Deputy Collector,	1	
U.S. Gauger,	1	
U.S. Postmasters,	2	
U.S. Clerks,	44	
State Civil Service, 2	2	
City Civil Service, 1	1	Total 53
Business Men:		
Merchants, etc.,	30	
Managers,	13	
Real Estate Dealers,	4	Total 47
Farmers		26
Clerks and Secretaries		
Secretary of National Societies,	7	
Clerks, etc.,	15	Total 22
Artisans		9
Editors		9
Miscellaneous		5

These figures illustrate vividly the function of the college-bred Negro. He is, as he ought to be, the group leader, the man who sets the ideals of the community where he lives, directs its thoughts and heads its social movements. It need hardly be argued that the Negro people need social leadership more than most groups; that they have no traditions to fall back upon, no long established customs, no strong family ties, no well defined social classes. All these things must be slowly and painfully evolved. The preacher was, even before the war, the group leader of the Negroes, and the church their greatest social institution. Naturally this preacher was ignorant and often immoral, and the problem of replacing the older type by better educated men has been a difficult one. Both by direct work and by direct influence on other preachers, and on congregations, the college-bred preacher has an opportunity for reformatory work and moral inspiration, the value of which cannot be overestimated.

It has, however, been in the furnishing of teachers that the Negro college has found its peculiar function. Few persons realize how vast a work, how mighty a revolution has been thus accomplished. To furnish five millions and more of ignorant people with teachers of their own race and blood, in one generation, was not only a very difficult undertaking, but very important one, in that, it placed before the eyes of almost every Negro child an attainable ideal. It brought the masses of the blacks in contact with modern civilization, made black men the leaders of their communities and trainers of the new generation. In this work college-bred Negroes were first teachers, and then teachers of teachers. And here it is that the broad culture of college work has been of peculiar value. Knowledge of life and its wider meaning, has been the point of the Negro's deepest ignorance, and the seeding out of teachers whose training has not been simply for bread winning, but also for human culture, has been of inestimable value in the training of these men.

In earlier years the two occupations of preacher and teacher were practically the only ones open to the black college graduate. Of later years a larger diversity of life among his people, has opened new avenues of employment. Nor have these college men been paupers and spendthrifts; 557 college-bred Negroes owned in 1899, $1,342,862.50 worth of real estate (assessed value), or $2,411 per family. The real value of the total accumulations of the whole group is perhaps about $10,000,000 or $5,000 apiece. Pitiful is it not beside the fortunes of oil kings and steel trusts, but after all is the fortune of the millionaire the only stamp of true and successful living? Alas! it is, with many and there's the rub.

The problem of training the Negro is to-day immensely complicated by the fact that the whole question of the efficiency and appropriateness of our present systems of education, for any kind of child, is a matter of active debate, in which final settlement seems still afar off. Consequently it often happens that persons arguing for or against certain systems of education for Negroes, have these controversies in mind and miss the real question at issue. The main question, so far as the Southern Negro is concerned, is: What under the present circumstance, must a system of education do in order to raise the Negro as quickly as possible in the scale of civilization? The answer to this question seems to me clear: It must strengthen the Negro's character, increase his knowledge and teach him to earn a living. Now it goes without saying that it is hard to do all these things simultaneously or suddenly and that at the same time it will not do to give all the attention to one and neglect the others; we could give black boys trades, but that alone will not civilize a race of ex-slaves; we might simply increase their knowledge of the world, but this would not necessarily make them wish to use this knowledge honestly; we might seek to strengthen character and purpose, but to what end if this people have nothing to eat or to wear? A system of education is not one thing, nor does it have a single definite object, nor is it a mere matter of schools. Education is that whole system of human training within and without the school house walls, which molds and develops men. If then we start out to train an ignorant and unskilled people with a heritage of bad habits, our system of training must set before itself two great aims—the one dealing with knowledge and character, the other part seeking to give the child the technical knowledge necessary for him to earn a living under the present circumstances.

These objects are accomplished in part by the opening of the common schools on the one, and of the industrial schools on the other. But only in part, for there must also be trained those who are to teach these schools—men and women of knowledge and culture and technical skill who understand modern civilization, and have the training and aptitude to impart it to the children under them. There must be teachers, and teachers of teachers, and to attempt to establish any sort of a system of common and industrial school training, without *first* (and I say *first* advisedly) without *first* providing for the higher training of the very best teachers, is simply throwing your money to the winds. School houses do not teach themselves—piles of brick and mortar and machinery do not send out *men*. It is the trained, living human soul, cultivated and strengthened by long study and thought, that breathes the real breath of life into boys and girls and makes them human, whether they be black or white, Greek, Russian or American. Nothing, in these latter days, has so dampened the faith of thinking Negroes in recent educational movements, as the fact that such movements have been accompanied by ridicule and denouncement and decrying of those very institutions of higher training which made the Negro public school possible, and make Negro industrial schools thinkable. It was: Fisk, Atlanta, Howard and Straight, those colleges born of the faith and sacrifice of the abolitionists, that placed in the black schools of the South the 30,000 teachers and more, which some, who depreciate the work of these higher schools, are using to teach their own new experiments. If Hampton, Tuskegee and the hundred other industrial schools prove in the future to be as successful as they deserve to be, then their success in training black artisans for the South, will be due primarily to the white colleges of the North and the black colleges of the South, which trained the teachers who to-day conduct these institutions. There was a time when the American people believed pretty devoutly that a log of wood with a boy at one end and Mark Hopkins at the other, represented the highest ideal of human training. But in these eager days it would seem that we have changed all that and think it necessary to add a couple of saw-mills and a hammer to this outfit, and, at a pinch, to dispense with the services of Mark Hopkins.

I would not deny, or for a moment seem to deny, the paramount necessity of teaching the Negro to work, and to work steadily and skillfully; or seem to depreciate in the slightest degree the important part industrial schools must play in the accomplishment of these ends, but I *do* say, and insist upon it, that it is industrialism drunk with its vision of success, to imagine that its own work can be accomplished without providing for the training of broadly cultured men and women to teach its own teachers, and to teach the teachers of the public schools.

But I have already said that human education is not simply a matter of schools; it is much more a matter of family and group life—the training of one's home, of one's daily companions, of one's social class. Now the black boy of the South moves in a black world—a world with its own leaders, its own thoughts, its own ideals. In this world he gets by far the larger part of his life training, and through the eyes of this dark world he peers into the veiled world beyond. Who guides and determines the education which he receives in his world? His teachers here are the group-leaders of the Negro people—the physicians and clergymen, the trained fathers and mothers, the influential and forceful men about him of all kinds; here it is, if at all, that the culture of the surrounding world trickles through and is handed on by the graduates of the higher schools. Can such culture training of group leaders be neglected? Can we afford to ignore it? Do you think that if the leaders of thought among Negroes are not trained and educated thinkers, that they will have no leaders? On the contrary a hundred half-trained demagogues will still hold the places they so largely occupy now, and hundreds of vociferous busy-bodies will multiply. You have no choice; either you must help furnish this race from within its own ranks with thoughtful men of trained leadership, or you must suffer the evil consequences of a headless misguided rabble.

I am an earnest advocate of manual training and trade teaching for black boys, and for white boys, too. I believe that next to the founding of Negro colleges the most valuable addition to Negro education since the war, has been industrial training for black boys. Nevertheless, I insist that the object of all true education is not to make men carpenters, it is to make carpenters men; there are two means of making the carpenter a man, each equally important: the first is to give the group and community in which he works, liberally trained teachers and leaders to teach him and his family what life means; the second is to give him sufficient intelligence and technical skill to make him an efficient workman; the first object demands the Negro college and college-bred men—not a quantity of such colleges, but a few of excellent quality; not too many college-bred men, but enough to leaven the lump, to inspire the masses, to raise the Talented Tenth to leadership; the second object demands a good system of common schools, well-taught, conveniently located and properly equipped.

The Sixth Atlanta Conference truly said in 1901:

"We call the attention of the Nation to the fact that less than one million of the three million Negro children of school age, are at present regularly attending school, and these attend a session which lasts only a few months.

"We are to-day deliberately rearing millions of our citizens in ignorance, and at the same time limiting the rights of citizenship by educational qualifications. This is unjust. Half the black youth of the land have no opportunities open to them for learning to read; write and cipher. In the discussion as to the proper training of Negro children after they leave the public schools, we have forgotten that they are not yet decently provided with public schools.

"Propositions are beginning to be made in the South to reduce the already meagre school facilities of Negroes. We congratulate the South on resisting, as much as it has, this pressure, and on the many millions it has spent on Negro education. But it is only fair to point out that Negro taxes and the Negroes' share of the income from indirect taxes and endowments have fully repaid this expenditure, so that the Negro public school system has not in all probability cost the white taxpayers a single cent since the war.

"This is not fair. Negro schools should be a public burden, since they are a public benefit. The Negro has a right to demand good common school training at the hands of the States and the Nation since by their fault he is not in position to pay for this himself."

What is the chief need for the building up of the Negro public school in the South? The Negro race in the South needs teachers to-day above all else. This is the concurrent testimony of all who know the situation. For the supply of this great demand two things are needed—institutions of higher education and money for school houses and salaries. It is usually assumed that a hundred or more institutions for Negro training are to-day turning out so many teachers and college-bred men that the race is threatened with an over-supply. This is sheer nonsense. There are to-day less than 3,000 living Negro college graduates in the United States, and less than 1,000 Negroes in college. Moreover, in the 164 schools for Negroes, 95 percent of their students are doing elementary and secondary work, work which should be done in the public schools. Over half the remaining 2,157 students are taking high school studies. The mass of so-called "normal" schools for the Negro, are simply doing elementary common school work, or, at most, high school work, with a little instruction in methods. The Negro colleges and the post-graduate courses at other institutions are the only agencies for the broader and more careful training of teachers. The work of these institutions is hampered for lack of funds. It is getting increasingly difficult to get funds for training teachers in the best modern methods, and yet all over the South, from State Superintendents, county officials, city boards and school principals comes the wail, "We need TEACHERS!" and teachers must be trained. As the fairest minded of all white Southerners, Atticus G. Haygood, once said: "The defects of colored teachers are so great as to create an urgent necessity for training better ones. Their excellencies and their successes are sufficient to justify the best hopes of success in the effort, and to vindicate the judgment of those who make large investments of money and service, to give to colored students opportunity for thoroughly preparing themselves for the work of teaching children of their people."

The truth of this has been strikingly shown in the marked improvement of white teachers in the South. Twenty years ago the rank and file of white public school teachers were not as good as the Negro teachers. But they, by scholarships and good salaries, have been encouraged to thorough normal and collegiate preparation, while the Negro teachers have been discouraged by starvation wages and the idea that any training will do for a black teacher. If carpenters are needed it is well and good to train men as carpenters. But to train men as carpenters, and then set them to teaching is wasteful and criminal; and to train men as teachers and then refuse them living wages, unless they become carpenters, is rank nonsense.

The United States Commissioner of Education says in his report for 1900: "For comparison between the white and colored enrollment in secondary and higher education, I have added together the enrollment in high schools and secondary schools, with the attendance on colleges and universities, not being sure of the actual grade of work done in the colleges and universities. The work done in the secondary schools is reported in such detail in this office, that there can be no doubt of its grade."

He then makes the following comparisons of persons in every million enrolled in secondary and higher education:

Year	Whole Country	Negros [sic]
1880	4,362	1,289
1900	10,743	2,061

And he concludes: "While the number in colored high schools and colleges had increased somewhat faster than the population, it had not kept pace with the average of the whole country, for it had fallen from 30 per cent to 24 per cent of the average quota. Of all-colored pupils; one (1) in one hundred was engaged in secondary and higher work, and that ratio has continued substantially for the past twenty years. If the ratio of colored population in secondary and higher education is to be equal to the average for the whole country, it must be increased to five times its present average." And if this be true of the secondary and higher education, it is safe to say that the Negro has not one-tenth his quota in college studies. How baseless, therefore, is the charge of too much training! We need Negro teachers for the Negro common schools, and we need first-class normal schools and colleges to train them. This is the work of higher Negro education and it must be done.

Further than this, after being provided with group leaders of civilization, and a foundation of intelligence in the public schools, the carpenter, in order to be a man, needs technical skill. This calls for trade schools. Now trade schools are not nearly such simple things as people once thought. The original idea was that the "Industrial" school was to furnish education, practically free, to those willing to work for it; it was to "do" things—i.e.: become a center of productive industry, it was to be partially, if not wholly, self-supporting, and it was to teach trades. Admirable as were some of the ideas underlying this scheme, the whole thing simply would not work in practice; it was found that if you were to use time and material to teach trades thoroughly, you could not at the same time keep the industries on a commercial basis and make them pay. Many schools started out to do this on a large scale and went into virtual bankruptcy.

Moreover, it was found also that it was possible to teach a boy a trade mechanically, without giving him the full educative benefit of the process, and, vice versa, that there was a distinctive educative value in teaching a boy to use his hands and eyes in carrying out certain physical processes, even though he did not actually learn a trade. It has happened, therefore, in the last decade, that a noticeable change has come over the industrial schools. In the first place the idea of commercially remunerative industry in a school is being pushed rapidly to the background. There are still schools with shops and farms that bring an income and schools that use student labor partially for the erection of their buildings and the furnishing of equipment. It is coming to be seen, however, in the education of the Negro, as clearly as it has been seen in the education of the youths the world over, that it is the *boy* and not the material product, that is the true object of education.

Consequently the object of the industrial school came to be the thorough training of boys regardless of the cost of the training, so long as it was thoroughly well done.

Even at this point, however, the difficulties were not surmounted. In the first place modern industry has taken great strides since the war, and the teaching of trades is no longer a simple matter. Machinery and long processes of work have greatly changed the work of the carpenter, the ironworker and the shoemaker. A really efficient workman must be to-day an intelligent man who has had good technical training in addition to thorough common school, and perhaps even higher training. To meet this situation the industrial schools began a further development; they established distinct Trade Schools for the thorough training of better class artisans, and at the same time they sought to preserve for the purposes of general education, such of the simpler processes of elementary trade learning as were best suited therefor. In this differentiation of the Trade School and manual training, the best of the industrial schools simply followed the plain trend of the present educational epoch. A prominent educator tells us that, in Sweden, "In the beginning the economic conception was generally adopted, and everywhere manual, training was looked upon as a means of preparing the children of the common people to earn their living. But gradually it came to be recognized that manual training has a more elevated purpose, and one, indeed, more useful in the deeper meaning of the term. It came to be considered as an educative process for the complete moral, physical and intellectual development of the child."

Thus, again, in the manning of trade schools and manual training schools we are thrown back upon the higher training as its source and chief support. There was a time when any aged and worn out carpenter could teach in a trade school. But not so to-day. Indeed the demand for college-bred men by a school like

Tuskegee, ought to make Mr. Booker T. Washington the firmest friend of higher training.[23] Here he has as helpers the son of a Negro senator, trained in Greek and the humanities, and graduated at Harvard; the son of a Negro congressman and lawyer, trained in Latin and mathematics, and graduated at Oberlin; he has as his wife, a woman who read Virgil and Homer in the same class room with me; he has as college chaplain, a classical graduate of Atlanta University; as teacher of science, a graduate of Fisk; as teacher of history, a graduate of Smith,—indeed some thirty of his chief teachers are college graduates, and instead of studying French grammars in the midst of weeds, or buying pianos for dirty cabins, they are at Mr. Washington's right hand helping him in a noble work. And yet one of the effects of Mr. Washington's propaganda has been to throw doubt upon the expediency of such training for Negroes, as these persons have had.

Men of America, the problem is plain before you. Here is a race transplanted through the criminal foolishness of your fathers. Whether you like it or not the millions are here, and here they will remain. If you do not lift them up, they will pull you down. Education and work are the levers to uplift a people. Work alone will not do it unless inspired by the right ideals and guided by intelligence. Education must not simply teach work—it must teach

---

23   Du Bois applied for a faculty position in 1894 at Tuskegee, making a personal appeal to Booker T. Washington. Du Bois was offered a position in Mathematics days after accepting a teaching position in the Humanities at Wilberforce. Given Washington's knowledge of faculty hiring at Black colleges during that time, it is very likely that Washington was aware of the Wilberforce offer, when he replied to Du Bois.

The conflict between Washington and Du Bois reached a fevered pitch following the release of *The Souls of Black Folk*, particularly with the inclusion of the essay "Of Mr. Booker T. Washington and Others," in which Du Bois openly questioned Washington's intellect, and the legitimacy of his ascent to race leadership. Their rivalry, which ranged from friendly adversaries to bitter mistrust endured until Washington's death in 1915.

Life. The Talented Tenth of the Negro race must be made leaders of thought and missionaries of culture among their people. No others can do this work and Negro colleges must train men for it. The Negro race, like all other races, is going to be saved by its exceptional men.

THE TRAINING OF THE NEGRO FOR SOCIAL POWER (1903)[24]

The responsibility for their own social regeneration ought to be placed largely upon the shoulders of the negro people. But such responsibility must carry with it a grant of power; responsibility without power is a mockery and a farce. If, therefore the American people are sincerely anxious that the negro shall put forth his best efforts to help himself, they must see to it that he is not deprived of the freedom and power to strive. The responsibility for dispelling their own ignorance implies that the power to, overcome ignorance is to be placed in black men's hands; the lessening of poverty calls for the power of effective work; and the responsibility for lessening crime calls for control over social forces which produce crime.

Such social power means, assuredly, the growth of initiative among negroes, the spread of independent thought, the expanding consciousness of manhood; and these things today are looked upon by many with apprehension and distrust, and there is systematic and determined effort to avoid this inevitable corollary of the fixing of social responsibility. Men openly declare their design to train these millions as a subject

---

24 Originally appeared in *The Outlook*, October 17, 1903.

caste, as men to be thought for, but not to think; to be led, but not to lead themselves.

Those who advocate these things forget that such a solution flings them squarely on the other horn of the dilemma: such a subject child-race could never be held accountable for its own misdeeds and shortcomings; its ignorance would be part of the Nation's design, its poverty would arise partly from the direct oppression of the strong and partly from thriftlessness which such oppression breeds; and, above all, its crime would be the legitimate child of "that lack of self-respect which caste systems engender. Such a solution of the Negro problem is not one which the saner sense of the Nation for a moment contemplates; it is utterly foreign to American institutions, and is unthinkable as a future for any self-respecting race of men. The sound afterthought of the American people must come to realize that the responsibility for dispelling ignorance" and poverty and uprooting crime among negroes cannot be put upon their own shoulders unless; they are given such independent leadership in intelligence; skill, and morality—as will inevitably lead to an independent manhood which cannot and will not rest in bonds.

Let me illustrate my meaning particularly in the matter of educating negro youth.

The negro problem, it has often been said, is largely a problem of ignorance—not simply of illiteracy, but a deeper ignorance of the world and its ways, of the thought and experience of men; an ignorance of self and the possibilities of human souls. This can be gotten rid of only by training; and primarily such training must take the form of that sort of social leadership which we call education. To apply such leadership to themselves, and to profit by it, means that negroes would have among themselves men of careful training and broad culture, as teachers and teachers of teachers. There are always periods of educational evolution when it is deemed quite proper for pupils in the fourth reader to teach those in the third. But such a method, wasteful and ineffective at all times, is peculiarly dangerous when ignorance is widespread and when there are few homes and public institutions to supplement the work of the school. It is, therefore, of crying necessity among negroes that the heads of their educational system—the teachers in the normal schools, the heads of high schools, the principals of public systems, should be unusually well trained men; men trained not simply in common-school branches, not simply in the technique of school management and normal methods, but trained beyond this, broadly and carefully, into the meaning of the age whose civilization it is their peculiar duty to interpret to the youth of a new race, to the minds of untrained people. Such educational leaders should be prepared by long and rigorous courses. I of study similar to those which the world over have been designed to strengthen ; the intellectual powers, fortify character, and facilitate the transmission from age to age of the stores of the world's knowledge.

Not all men—indeed, not the majority of men, only the exceptional few among American negroes or among any other people—are adapted to this higher training, as, indeed, only the exceptional few are adapted to higher training in any line; but the significance of such, men is not to be measured by their numbers, but rather by the numbers of their pupils and followers who are destined to see the world through their eyes, hear it through their trained ears, and speak to it through the music of their words.

Such men, teachers of teachers and leaders of the untaught, Atlanta University and similar colleges seek to train. We seek to do our work thoroughly and carefully. We have no predilections or prejudices as to particular studies or methods, but we do cling to those time-honored sorts of discipline which the experience of the world has long since proven to be of especial value. We sift as carefully as possible the student material which offers itself, and we try by every conscientious, method to give to students who have character and ability such years of discipline as shall make them stronger, keener, and better for their peculiar mission. The history of civilization seems to prove that no group or nation which seeks advancement and true development can despise or neglect the power of well-trained minds; and this power of intellectual leadership must be given to the talented tenth among American negroes before this race can seriously be asked to assume the responsibility of dispelling its own ignorance. Upon the foundation-stone of a few well equipped negro colleges of high and honest standards can be built a proper system of free common schools in the South for the masses of the negro people; any attempt to found a system of public schools on anything less than this—on narrow ideals, limited or merely technical training—is to call blind leaders for the blind.

The very first step toward the settlement of the negro problem is the spread of intelligence. The step toward wider intelligence is a free public-school system; and the first and most important step toward a public-school system is the equipment and adequate support of a sufficient number of negro colleges. These are first steps, and they involve great movements: first, the best of the existent colleges must not be abandoned to slow atrophy and death, as the tendency is to-day; secondly, systematic attempt must be made to organize secondary education, Below the colleges and connected with them must come the normal and high schools, judiciously distributed and carefully manned. In no essential particular should this system of common and secondary schools differ from educational systems the world over. Their chief function is the quickening and training of human intelligence; they can do much in the teaching of morals and manners incidentally, but they cannot and ought not to replace the home as the chief moral teacher; they can teach valuable lessons as to the meaning of work in the world, but they cannot replace technical schools and apprenticeship in actual life, which are the real schools of work. Manual training can and ought to be used in these schools, but as a means and not as an end—to quicken intelligence and self-knowledge and not to teach carpentry just as arithmetic is used to train minds and not skilled accountants.

Whence, now, is the money coming for this educational system? For the common schools the support should come from local communities, the State governments, and the United States Government; for secondary education, support should come from local and State governments and private philanthropy; for the colleges from private philanthropy and the United States Government. I make no apology for bringing the United States Government in thus conspicuously. The General Government must give aid to Southern education if illiteracy and ignorance are to cease threatening the very foundations of civilization within, any reasonable time. Aid to common-school education could be appropriated to the different States on the basis of illiteracy. The fund could be administered by State officials, and the results and needs reported upon by United States educational inspectors under the Bureau of Education. The States could easily distribute the funds so as to encourage local taxation and enterprise and not result in pauperizing the communities. As to higher training, it must be remembered that the cost of a single battleship like the Massachusetts would endow all the distinctively college work necessary for negroes during the next half-century; and it is without doubt true that the unpaid balance from bounties withheld from negroes in the Civil War would, with interest, easily supply this sum.

But spread of intelligence alone will not solve the negro problem. If this problem is largely a question of ignorance, it is also scarcely

119

less a problem of poverty. If negroes are to assume the responsibility of raising the standards of living among themselves, the power of intelligent work and leadership toward proper industrial ideals must be placed in their bands. Economic efficiency depends on intelligence, skill, and thrift. The public-school system is designed to furnish the necessary intelligence for the ordinary worker, the secondary school for the more gifted workers, and the college for the exceptional few. Technical knowledge and manual dexterity in learning branches of the world's work are taught industrial and trade schools and such schools are of prime importance in the training of colored children. Trade-teaching cannot be effectively combined with the work of the common schools because the primary curriculum is already too crowded, and thorough common-school training should precede trade-teaching. It is, however, quite possible to combine some of the work of the secondary schools with purely technical training, the necessary limitations being matters of time and cost: the question whether the boy can afford to stay in school long enough to add parts of a high-school course to the trade course, and particularly the question whether the school can afford or ought to afford to give trade-training to high-school students who do not intend to become artisans. A system of trade-schools, therefore, supported by State and private aid, should be added to the secondary school system.

An industrial school, however, does not merely teach technique. It is also a school—a center of moral influence and of mental discipline. As such it has peculiar problems in securing the proper teaching force. It demands broadly trained men: the teacher of carpentry must be more than a carpenter, and the teacher of the domestic arts more than a cook; for such teachers must instruct, not simply in manual dexterity, but in mental quickness and moral habits. In other words, they must be teachers as well as artisans. It thus happens that college-bred men and men from other higher schools have always been in demand in technical schools, and it has been the high privilege of Atlanta University to furnish during the thirty-six years of its existence a part of the teaching force of nearly every negro industrial school in the United States, and to-day our graduates are teaching in more than twenty such institutions. The same might be said of Fisk University and other higher schools. If the college graduates were to-day withdrawn from the teaching force of the chief negro industrial schools, nearly every one of them would have to close its doors. These facts are forgotten by such advocates of industrial training as oppose the higher schools. Strong as the argument for industrial schools is—and its strength is undeniable—its cogency simply increases the urgency of the plea for higher training-schools and colleges to furnish broadly educated teachers.

But intelligence and skill alone will not solve the Southern problem of poverty. With these must go that combination of homely habits and virtues which we may loosely call thrift. Something of thrift may be taught in school, more must be taught at home; but both these agencies are helpless when organized economic society denies to workers the just rewards of thrift and efficiency. And this has been true of black laborers in the South from the time of slavery down through the scandal of the Freedmen's Bank to the peonage and crop-lien system of to-day. If the Southern negro is shiftless, it is primarily because over large areas a shiftless negro can get on in the world about as well as an industrious black man. This is not universally true in the South, but it is true to so large an extent as to discourage striving in precisely that class of negroes who most need encouragement. What is the remedy? Intelligence—not simply the ability to read and write or to sew—but the intelligence of a society permeated by that larger vision of life and broader tolerance which are fostered by the college and university. Not that all men must be college-bred, but that some men, black and white, must be, to leaven the ideals of the lump. Can any serious student of the economic South doubt that this to-day is her crying need?

Ignorance and poverty are the vastest of the negro problems. But to these later years have added a third—the problem of negro crime. That a great problem of social morality must have become eventually the central problem of emancipation is as clear as day to any student of history. In its grosser form as a problem of serious crime it is already upon us. Of course it is false and silly to represent that white women in the South are in daily danger of black assaulters. On the contrary, white womanhood in the South is absolutely safe in the hands of ninety-five per cent of the black men—ten times safer than black womanhood is in the hands of white men. Nevertheless, there is a large and dangerous class of negro criminals, paupers, and outcasts. The existence and growth of such a class, far from causing surprise, should be recognized as the natural result of that social disease called the negro problem nearly every untoward circumstance known to human experience has united to increase negro crime: the slavery of the past, the sudden emancipation, the narrowing of economic opportunity, the lawless environment of wide regions, the stifling of natural ambition, the curtailment of political privilege, the disregard of the sanctity of black men's homes, and, above all, a system of treatment for criminals calculated to breed crime far faster than all other available agencies could repress it. Such a combination of circumstances is as sure to increase the numbers of the vicious and outcast as the rain is to wet the earth. The phenomenon calls for no delicately drawn theories of race differences; it is a plain case of cause and effect.

But, plain as the causes may be, the results are just as deplorable, and repeatedly to-day the criticism is made that negroes do not recognize sufficiently their responsibility in this matter. Such critics forget how little power to-day negroes have over their own lower classes. Before the black murderer who strikes his victim to-day, the average black man stands far more helpless than the average white, and, too, suffers ten times more from the effects of the deed. The white man has political power, accumulated wealth, and knowledge of social forces; the black man is practically disfranchised, poor, and unable to discriminate between the criminal and the martyr. The negro needs the defense of the ballot, the conserving power of property, and, above all, the ability to cope intelligently with such vast questions of social regeneration and moral reform as confront him. If social reform among negroes be without organization or trained leadership from within, if the administration of law is always for the avenging of the white victim and seldom for the reformation of the black criminal, if ignorant black men misunderstand the functions of government because they have had no decent instruction, and intelligent black men are denied a voice in government because they are black—under such circumstances to hold negroes responsible for the suppression of crime among themselves is the cruelest of mockeries.

On the other hand, a sincere desire among the American people to help the negroes undertake their own social regeneration means, first, that the negro be given ballot on the same terms as other men, to protect him against injustice and to safeguard his interests in the administration of law; secondly, that through education and social organization he be trained to work, and save, and earn a decent living. But these are not all; wealth is not the only thing worth accumulating; experience and knowledge can be accumulated and handed down, and no people can be truly rich without them. Can the negro do without these? Can this training in work and thrift be truly effective without the guidance of trained intelligence and deep knowledge without that same efficiency which has enabled modern peoples to grapple so successfully with the problems of the Submerged Tenth? There must surely be among negro leaders the philanthropic impulse, the uprightness of character and strength of purpose, but there must be more than these; philanthropy and purpose among blacks as well as among whites must be guided and curbed by knowledge and mental discipline—knowledge of the forces of civilization that make for survival, ability to organize and guide those forces, and realization of the true meaning of those broader ideals of human betterment which may in time bring heaven and earth a little nearer. This is social power—it is gotten in many ways by experience, by social contact, by what we loosely call the chances of life. But the systematic method of acquiring and imparting it is by the training of youth to thought, power and knowledge in school and college. And that group of people whose mental grasp is by heredity weakest, and whose knowledge of the past is for historic reasons most imperfect, that group is the very one which needs above all, for the talented of its youth, this severe and careful course of training; especially if they are expected to take immediate part in modern competitive life, if they are to hasten the slower courses of human development, and if the responsibility for this is to be in their own hands.

Three things American slavery gave the negro—the habit of work, the English language, and the Christian religion; but one priceless thing it debauched, destroyed, and took from him, and that was the organized home. For the sake of intelligence and thrift, for the sake of work and morality, this home-life must be restored and regenerated with newer ideals. How? The normal method would be by actual contact with a higher home-life among his neighbors, but this method the social separation of white and black precludes. A proposed method is by schools of domestic arts, but, valuable as these are, they are but subsidiary aids to the establishment of homes; for real homes are primarily centers of ideals and teaching and only incidentally centers of cooking. The restoration and raising of home ideals must, then, come from social life among negroes themselves; and does that social life need no leadership? It needs the best possible leadership of pure hearts and trained heads, the highest leadership of carefully trained men.

Such are the arguments for the negro college, and such is the work that Atlanta University and a few similar institutions seek to do. We believe that a rationally arranged college course of study for men and women able to pursue it is the best and only method of putting into the world negroes with ability to use the social forces of their race so as to stamp out crime, strengthen the home, eliminate degenerates, and inspire and encourage the higher tendencies of the race not only in thought and aspiration but in every-day toil. And we believe this, not simply because we have argued that such training ought to have these effects, or merely because we hope for such results in some dim future, but because already for years we have seen in the work of our graduates precisely such results as I have mentioned: successful teachers of teachers, intelligent and upright ministers, skilled physicians, principals of industrial schools, business men, and, above all, makers of model homes and leaders of social groups, out from which radiate subtle but tangible forces of uplift and inspiration. The proof of this lies scattered in every State of the South, and, above all, in the half-unwilling testimony of men disposed to decry our work.

Between the negro college and industrial school there are the strongest grounds for co-operation and unity. It is not a matter of mere emphasis, for we would be glad to see ten industrial schools to every college. It is not a fact that there are to-day too few negro colleges, but rather that there are too many institutions attempting to do college work. But the danger lies in the fact that the best of the negro colleges are poorly equipped and are to-day losing support and countenance, and that, unless the Nation awakens to its duty, ten years will see the annihilation of higher negro training in the South. We need a few strong, well-equipped negro colleges, and we need them now, not tomorrow; unless we can have them and have them decently supported, negro education in the South, both common-school and industrial, is doomed to failure, and the forces of social regeneration will be fatally weakened, for the college to-day among negroes is, just as truly as it was yesterday among whites, the beginning and not the end of human training, the foundation and not the capstone of popular education.

Strange, is it not, my brothers, how often in America those great watch-words of human energy—"Be strong!" "Know thyself" "Hitch your wagon to a star!"—how often these die away into dim whispers when we face these seething millions of black men? And yet do they not belong to them? Are they not their heritage as well as yours? Can they bear burdens without strength, know without learning, and aspire without ideals? Are you afraid to let them try? Fear rather, in this our common fatherland, lest we live to lose those great watchwords of Liberty and Opportunity which yonder in the eternal hills their fathers fought with your fathers to preserve.

Section III

ABLE TO LEAD THE WORLD
Reconsidering the Role of Black Education
1914-1948

Video Sidebar

Westbrook describes the third section of
EDUCATION AND EMPOWERMENT.

http://youtu.be/HbwpMMM-xSY

CREDO[25] (1904)

I believe in God who made of one blood all races that dwell on earth. I believe that all men, black and brown and white, are brothers, varying through Time and Opportunity, in form and gift and feature, but differing in no essential particular, and alike in soul and in the possibility of infinite development.

Especially do I believe in the Negro Race; in the beauty of its genius, the sweetness of its soul and its strength in that meekness which shall yet inherit this turbulent earth.

I believe in pride of race and lineage and self; in pride of self so deep as to scorn injustice to other selves; in pride of lineage so great as to despise no man's father; in pride of race so chivalrous as neither to offer bastardy to the weak nor beg wedlock of the strong, knowing that men may be brothers in Christ, even they be not brothers-in-law.

I believe in Service—humble reverent service, from the blackening of boots to the whitening of souls; for Work is Heaven, Idleness Hell, and Wage is the "Well done!" of the Master who summoned all them that labor and are heavy laden, making no distinction between the black sweating cotton-hands of Georgia and the First Families of Virginia, since all distinction not, based on deed is devilish and not divine.

I believe in the Devil and his angels, who wantonly work to narrow the opportunity of struggling human beings, especially if they be, black; who spit in the faces of the fallen, strike them that cannot strike again, believe the worst and work to prove it, hating the image which their Maker stamped on a brother's soul.

I believe in the Prince of Peace. I believe that War is Murder. I believe that armies and navies are at bottom the tinsel and braggadocio of oppression and wrong; and I believe that the wicked

---

25   Originally appeared in *Independent, 57.* (October 6, 1904): 787.

conquest of weaker and darker nations by nations whiter and stronger but foreshadows the death of that strength.

I believe in Liberty for all men; the space to stretch their arms and their souls; the right to breathe and the right to vote, the freedom to choose their friends, enjoy the sunshine and ride on the railroads, uncursed by color; thinking; dreaming, working as they will in a kingdom of God and love.

I believe in the training of children, black even as white; the leading out of little souls into the green pastures and beside the still waters, not for self or peace, but for then, shall we do? Give up the training of black men, or cheapen it, or train them simply as "hands"? No; let us be honest and straightforward, and realize that if making men better, wiser, and more ambitious brings "problems," then let the problems come, and let good men try to solve them righteously rather than to avoid them.

NIAGARA MOVEMENT SPEECH (1906)

The men of the Niagara Movement coming from the toil of the year's hard work and pausing a moment from the earning of their daily bread turn toward the nation and again ask in the name of ten million the privilege of a hearing. In the past year the work of the Negro hater has flourished in the land. Step by step the defenders of the rights of American citizens have retreated. The work of stealing the black man's ballot has progressed and the fifty and more representatives of stolen votes still sit in the nation's capital. Discrimination in travel and public accommodation has so spread that some of our weaker brethren are actually afraid to thunder against color discrimination as such and are simply whispering for ordinary decencies.

Against this the Niagara Movement eternally protests. We will not be satisfied to take one jot or tittle less than our full manhood rights. We claim for ourselves every single right that belongs to a freeborn American, political, civil and social; and until we get these rights we will never cease to protest and assail the ears of America. The battle we wage is not for ourselves alone but for all true Americans. It is a fight for ideals, lest this, our common fatherland, false to its founding, become in truth the land of the thief and the home of the Slave—a by-word and a hissing among the nations for its sounding pretensions and pitiful accomplishment.

Never before in the modern age has a great and civilized folk threatened to adopt so cowardly a creed in the treatment of its fellow-citizens born and bred on its soil. Stripped of verbiage and subterfuge and in its naked nastiness the new American creed says: Fear to let black men even try to rise lest they become the equals of the white. And this is the land that professes to follow Jesus Christ. The blasphemy of such a course is only matched by its cowardice.

In detail our demands are clear and unequivocal. First, we would vote; with the right to vote goes everything: Freedom, manhood, the honor of your wives, the chastity of your daughters, the right to work, and the chance to rise, and let no man listen to those who deny this.

We want full manhood suffrage, and we want it now, henceforth and forever.

Second. We want discrimination in public accommodation to cease. Separation in railway and street cars, based simply on race and color, is un-American, un-democratic, and silly. We protest against all such discrimination.

Third. We claim the right of freemen to walk, talk, and be with them that wish to be with us. No man has a right to choose another man's friends, and to attempt to do so is an impudent interference with the most fundamental human privilege.

Fourth. We want the laws enforced against rich as well as poor; against Capitalist as well as Laborer; against white as well as black. We are not more lawless than the white race, we are more often arrested, convicted, and mobbed. We want justice even for criminals and outlaws. We want the Constitution of the country enforced. We want Congress to take charge of Congressional elections. We want the Fourteenth amendment carried out to the letter and every State disfranchised in Congress which attempts to disfranchise its rightful voters. We want the Fifteenth amendment enforced and No State allowed to base its franchise simply on color.

The failure of the Republican Party in Congress at the session just closed to redeem its pledge of 1904 with reference to suffrage conditions at the South seems a plain, deliberate, and premeditated breach of promise, and stamps that party as guilty of obtaining votes under false pretense.

Fifth, We want our children educated. The school system in the country districts of the South is a disgrace and in few towns and cities are Negro schools what they ought to be. We want the national government to step in and wipe out illiteracy in the South. Either the United States will destroy ignorance or ignorance will destroy the United States.

And when we call for education we mean real education. We believe in work. We ourselves are workers, but work is not necessarily education. Education is the development of power and ideal. We want our children trained as intelligent human beings should be, and we will fight for all time against any proposal to educate black boys and girls simply as servants and underlings, or simply for the use of other people. They have a right to know, to think, to aspire.

These are some of the chief things which we want. How shall we get them? By voting where we may vote, by persistent, unceasing agitation; by hammering at the truth, by sacrifice and work.

We do not believe in violence, neither in the despised violence of the raid nor the lauded violence of the soldier, nor the barbarous violence of the mob, but we do believe in John Brown, in that incarnate spirit of justice, that hatred of a lie, that willingness to sacrifice money, reputation, and life itself on the altar of right. And here on the scene of John Brown's martyrdom we reconsecrate ourselves, our honor, our property to the final emancipation of the race which John Brown died to make free.

Our enemies, triumphant for the present, are fighting the stars in their courses. Justice and humanity must prevail. We live to tell these dark brothers of ours—scattered in counsel, wavering and weak—that no bribe of money or notoriety, no promise of wealth or fame, is worth the surrender of a people's manhood or the loss of a man's self-respect. We refuse to surrender the leadership of this race to cowards and trucklers. We are men; we will be treated as men. On this rock we have planted our banners. We will never give up, though the trump of doom finds us still fighting.

And we shall win. The past promised it, the present foretells it. Thank God for John Brown! Thank God for Garrison and Douglass! Sumner and Phillips, Nat Turner and Robert Gould Shaw, and all the hallowed dead who died for freedom! Thank God for all those to-day, few though their voices be, who have not forgotten the divine brotherhood of all men white and black, rich and poor, fortunate and unfortunate.

We appeal to the young men and women of this nation, to those whose nostrils are not yet befouled by greed and snobbery and racial narrowness: Stand up for the right, prove yourselves worthy of your heritage and whether born north or south dare to treat men as men. Cannot the nation that has absorbed ten million foreigners into its political life without catastrophe absorb ten million Negro Americans into that same political life at less cost than their unjust and illegal exclusion will involve?

Courage brothers! The battle for humanity is not lost or losing. All across the skies sit signs of promise. The Slav is raising in his might, the yellow millions are tasting liberty, the black Africans are writhing toward the light, and everywhere the laborer, with ballot in his hand, is voting open the gates of Opportunity and Peace. The morning breaks over blood-stained hills. We must not falter, we may not shrink. Above are the everlasting stars.

N.A.A.C.P. Fourth Annual Report [Excerpt] (1914)[26]

I t is now nearly a quarter of a century since the South presented to the nation a new and plausible method of settling the Negro problem. The argument is familiar to all: "Take the Negro out of politics; train him for work and particularly for farm work. The result will be the disappearance of the Negro problem." This prophecy has not been fulfilled.

Disfranchisement has been carried through ruthlessly. In Louisiana, for instance, less than 1 per cent of the colored men 21 years of age are registered, although over half of the Negro population in that State can read and write. This situation is typical of most of the gulf States. In the border States a larger number vote, but still the great majority of adult male Negroes are disfranchised in the South.

It was promised that in return for such disfranchisement the Negro was to have educational and economic rights.

The last study of "The Negro Common School" made by Atlanta University sums up the Negro educational situation by saying:

That the overwhelming majority of Negro children of school age are not in school.

1. That the chief reason for this is the lack of school facilities; and a further reason is the poverty and ignorance of parents.

2. That those Negro children who are in school are, as a

---

26   Du Bois cited the *Atlanta University Studies*, which he led and edited from 1897–1916. His connection with both the university and the NAACP remained strong until his resignation from the NAACP in 1948.

rule, poorly taught by half-prepared and poorly paid teachers and through short terms of three to six months a year.

3. That the schoolhouses and equipment for Negro schools are for the most part wretched and inadequate.

4. That the Negro schools, as a rule, receive little or no helpful superintendence from the school authorities.

5. That the result and apparently one of the objects of disfranchisement has been to cut down the Negro school fund, bar out competent teachers, lower the grade and efficiency of the course of study, and employ as teachers in the Negro schools those willing tools who do not and will not protest or complain.

6. That in the attempt to introduce much needed and valuable manual and industrial training there has been introduced into the curriculum of the Negro common school a mass of ill-considered, unrelated work, which has overburdened the teacher and pushed into the background the vital studies of reading, writing and arithmetic. In a large measure this has been done with the avowed object of training Negroes as menials and laborers and of cutting them off from the higher avenues of life.

7. That the forward movement in education in the South during the last ten years has been openly confined almost entirely to white people. The movement for local school taxes, better high schools, consolidation of schools and transportation of children has, with small exception, been encouraged and made possible among the whites and not among the Ne-

groes. In many cases the Negroes have been taxed for the improvement of white school facilities, while their own schools have not been allowed to share in these improvements.

8. That along with this curtailment of elementary public education for Negroes has gone a tendency to decry the work of those schools which are devoted to the higher training of the Negro youth, to lower their curricula, to cut off Northern benevolence and to decrease the supply of intellectual leaders for the Negro race.

Even with these patent facts staring the nation in the face most people have come to the idea that at least the economic rights of the Negro are secure, and many have been willing to say not only, "Give up the ballot," but also, "Give up educational ideals, so long as the race learns to work efficiently and accumulate property, particularly as farmers." Let us now ask what have been the results here?

So far as work is concerned we again find the barriers up and not tending to fall. The attempt to establish a strict caste of occupations in the South has not been successful, but it has been possible to keep the majority of Negroes in the most disagreeable and poorest-paid occupations, and in the lowest positions of most occupations. The Negro has pushed his way into some skilled occupations, but it has been a long and tedious fight. It is therefore wrong to assume that economic opportunity has been opened to the Negro with any great degree of freedom. But this is true: The South has been advancing in wealth at a phenomenal rate during the last two or three decades. It has been impossible, particularly in cities, to withhold some of the economic advantages of this great advance from the colored workers. The result has been a great increase of property holding among Negroes in cities and towns.

Unfortunately there are no complete figures to illustrate this as a whole, but a few facts and localities throw some light upon it. The property of the Negro church situated chiefly in Negro cities increased 115 per cent between 1890 and 1906. The town and city property of the Negroes of Georgia increased nearly 100 per cent between 1890 and 1907. In Virginia the town and city property of colored people increased from an assessed value of four million in 1899 to nine and one-half million in 1911. There is reason to believe that throughout the United States the increase of Negro city property has been very large in the last ten years.

The chief reason for this conclusion is unfortunately the increase of the city segregation movement. In other words, just as soon as the Negro city laborer, working on a wage scale lower than that of any other single group of people, saved out of his meagre [sic] earnings enough to move out of the alleys and slums to the front streets, there immediately arose the question as to who should bear the economic cost of race prejudice. Most people in their careless indulgence in race prejudice forget this economic cost. It shows itself in the social cost of crime, prostitution and slums, and it shows itself in the fall of values when a socially despised group moves into a decent neighborhood. That such a movement results in a real financial loss no one denies or attempts to deny. But the question is who shall bear the loss?

This segregation movement, as illustrated in Baltimore and many other Southern cities, and as advocated in St. Louis, answers this problem plainly. It proposed to put the whole cost of this economic loss absolutely upon the Negroes. That this is unjust goes without saying. They, of all parties, are the ones who should be exempt from any loss. But even here it has not been altogether easy to gain the sympathy of right-minded Americans. They have said: "It is largely a social matter," and "Let the Negroes develop their own settlements," forgetting the absolute injustice and preposterous demand which such an attitude makes. A further argument is, however: "Let the Negro stop crowding into the cities. Here they have in the country and in the South a wonderful chance for development. They can get hold of land; they know how to raise a great staple crop and many auxiliary crops. Here is an open economic field; let them take advantage of it."

It must not be thought that the Negroes themselves or their friends have been unaware of the economic chance of the Negro in Southern agriculture, but they have been trying to say that even in the country the economic man of to-day must be backed by social and political rights, else the fruit of his labor is not safe.

I doubt if in modern economic history the truth of this proposition has been more clearly proven than in the recent history of the Negro race in America. Here is a people which has been asked to give up its political and social rights in order to achieve economic freedom.

Despite the protest of a few far-seeing men among them the race has virtually done this. They have let themselves be deprived of the vote almost without a struggle, and they have openly and slavishly acknowledged that they are not fit associates for their fellow men, and they have hoped by reason of this craven surrender to earn a living, accumulate property and achieve finally the recognition of their fellow men. The result has been that their educational opportunities have been curtailed rather than expanded. Their right to work has been admitted but slowly and grudgingly among all but the lowest and worst-paid occupations. And their right to accumulate property in cities is threatened to-day with serious curtailment. With this astonishing record as an answer to the program of twenty years ago, what is the present situation of the Negro with regard to agricultural land in the South? Here, indeed, we reach the last boundaries in the question. Let us bring to mind once more what has been said and promised in the past.

The movement fathered by men like the late Morris K. Jesup and Robert Ogden stated to the world and said with conviction: "You have here 10,000,000 inferior folk. You have got to stop treating them like ordinary white humanity and treat them as Negroes. You must educate them for work, and particularly for farm labor, and when you do that you will find the white South meeting you more than half way and willing to agree to accord the Negroes every economic right which they deserve." Not only did the overwhelming public opinion of the North believe and acknowledge this policy, but many colored people acquiesced in it with enthusiasm.

Consequently the movement toward farm life among Negroes in the last decade has been phenomenal. While farms conducted by white farmers have increased 9 ½ per cent between 1900 and 1910, farms conducted by colored farmers have increased nearly 20 per cent. There were 7 ½ per cent more white farmers conducting their farms in 1910 than in 1900, but there were 17 per cent more colored owners conducting their farms. The land in Negro farms increased from 42,000,000 to 47,000,000 acres in that time, and the land in the hands of Negro farm Owners from 16,000,000 to 19,000,000 acres. To-day 29 per cent of the farms in the South are conducted by colored men, not counting the vast number of farms conducted by white men with colored labor. This would seem to be most encouraging, and especially so when we remember under what difficulties it has been accomplished.

In the country the disfranchisement of the Negro was completest; in the country the task idea of slavery lasted longest, and in the country new legislation did everything it could to reduce the black farmhand into peonage. To-day in many rural districts of the Gulf States the refusal of a colored man to work for a white man on any terms which the white man wishes to make can without great difficulty be made a penitentiary offence and the colored man sent as a slave of the State to work in chains for a large part of his natural life.

The revolt of the black laborer, however, makes this program impossible. He could not strike for higher wages, but he could run away to town, and he did in such numbers that labor scarcity was the cry of the plantations, and harsh contract and vagrancy laws were passed. The most effective bait, however, to keep the laborer was to sell him land on installments. In nine cases out of ten he was unable to keep his contract and remained a laborer. But in the tenth case he got his land. Sometimes he was helped by the better class landlords, by his relatives in the North, by the breaking up of big plantations, and in a few cases by philanthropy.

In these ways the value of the farm property owned by Negroes between 1900 and 1910 increased from $108,000,000 to $440,000,000, or about 400 per cent. During this same time the farm property of whites throughout the country increased but 93 per cent and the farm property of Southern whites increased 108 per cent. This increase in value is shown in the land, which went from $102,000,000 to $277,000,000, or 166 per cent; in the buildings, which went from $29,000,000 to $69,000,000, or 242 per cent; in implements and machinery, which went from $8,000,000 to $16,000,000, or 100 per cent, and in livestock, which increased 92 per cent, or from $41,000,000 to $78,000.000.

Negro land ownership has increased from about 3,000,000 acres in 1875 to 6,000,000 acres in 1880, to 8,000,000 acres in 1890, to 15,000,000 in 1900, and nearly 20,000,000 in 1910.

This is most gratifying, and if the prophets of the past were correct we would expect to hear a chorus of congratulation and good will from the best friends of the Negro in the South. We would expect an argument something like this: "You see, we have kept our word in the main issue. We have disfranchised the Negro, and while we have not given him large educational opportunity, and have kept him in his place in the industrial world, nevertheless, he has become a householder in the cities (although there we must limit him), and especially he has become fifty years after emancipation a landholder in the United States by his own unaided efforts. This shows the wisdom of our policy."

When, however, we come forward prepared to hear this argument and to answer its weak places, for it has weak places, we find on the part of the dominant South not only absence of all enthusiasm for this increase of Negro agricultural well-being, but a distinct air of disappointment and something worse. Indeed, this air of disappointment is so widespread that one cannot help wondering if the Negro has not been urged to take advantage of Southern agriculture just because some Southerners were convinced that he could not take such advantage, and that in the country districts of the South he could be held in his place politically, socially and economically.

It would be unfair to assume this without undoubted proof, and such proof comes to us unfortunately from North Carolina. In order to understand that development in North Carolina, let us just look at some significant figures.

Farms owned by Negroes in North Carolina have increased in the decade from 17,000 to 21,000, and the land from 965,000 acres to 1,200,000 acres; not only has there been this numerical increase, but while all farm property in North Carolina increased 130 per cent. Negro farm property increased 300 per cent, or from $9,000,000 to $27,000,000; and the value of the land alone increased from $5,000,000 to $17,000,000, or 320 per cent.

Has this caused any rejoicing in North Carolina? I regret to say it has not. On the contrary, it has led to widespread proposal for the most vital attack on the economic rights of the Negro ever put forward in the United States. Let no one misconceive the significance of this. The Negro was asked to give up his political rights for the sake of advance. He finds that with the giving up of his political rights his educational rights are curtailed, the right to work is increased but inadequately, his right to hold property in cities is being questioned, and now finally, there is a movement in the South to curtail his right to own agricultural land. This movement has not started with an ignorant agitator of the [Cole] Blease and [James K.] Vardaman and [Benjamin R.] Tillman type. Its sponsor is Clarence Poe, editor of the *Progressive Farmer*, and a man representing in many ways the best traditions of the South.

Mr. Poe began his campaign last summer in the *Progressive Farmer*, a weekly paper with a wide circulation among the most intelligent farmers all over the South. As a result of this campaign week after week, a growing mass of white farmers are crying with one of Poe's correspondents:

"North Carolina and the South for the white race should be the slogan from now henceforth."

Or as another says: "Mr. Clarence Poe's suggestions that the Negro buy land adjoining and settle in communities to themselves is a good one and will do more than anything else to adjust the race relations between the whites and blacks of the South. It is the 'Jim Crow' law put into effect in the rural districts."

Mr. Poe suggested that the Negro should be separated from the whites in the country districts by a law prohibiting future sale of land to him in white communities. His suggestion took immediate root, and a third correspondent writes: "Negro children are not allowed to attend school with whites; Negroes do not sit in the same cars, loaf in the same depots and feed at the same hotels as the white folks. Why, then, should landlords be allowed to impose them on white fanners and ruin entire sections of the country?"

Mr. Poe then began to carefully fortify and elaborate his original proposition:

"Everybody knows that the Negroes stand together. They are notoriously clannish in everything. They help one another even to the extent of shielding Negro criminals from the law.

"But while the Negroes have been pulling together in this way, what has been the attitude of our white people in the vital matters of saving the rural South to the white race? Everybody knows that the shameful and disgraceful fact is that the white people have not been pulling together, but that the white city land owner and merchant has too often practically taken sides against the struggling white tenant and small farmer and in favor of the Negro. I once said to a big plantation owner living in Memphis who had lands in Mississippi: 'What Mississippi needs is fewer big plantations cultivated by Negro tenants and more thrifty, enterprising, industrious white farmers—more white people. Why don't you try to get white tenants?' 'I don't want them,' he replied. 'They won't spend money and run accounts at our stores like the Negroes will, and, besides, they soon want to buy land themselves. The Negroes make more money for us.'"

A friend writes him elaborating this argument: "I believe the great trouble is with a certain class of white land owners. They have Negro tenants on their lands who are, in fact, really peons. They furnish their tenants everything in the spring at high rates and in the fall take everything at low rates. I have in mind a certain Negro who purchased a mule worth about $90 for $150, and after fifteen years of hard work the mule died without being paid for. In the meantime the white man got all the Negro made. Such land owners don't want intelligent white tenants. They want those whom they can use to their advantage. They are the ones who have sold land at exorbitant prices to Negroes thinking, perhaps, they could not pay for it."

Here is evidently a situation calling for remedy. A modern reformer would suggest the uprooting of peonage and the company-store system; co-operative buying of large tracts of land. But this remedy is far from these men's minds, and we discover that if the peon escapes and becomes an independent small farmer and land owner that he is, if anything, even more objectionable.

"The Negroes first ran us out because some white people moved to town, became merchants who furnished supplies for the Negro to make their crops, and now have sold their country land to them in farms containing twenty, thirty and forty acres, and occasionally 100 acres or more. They sometimes give them a long time for payment, the Negroes seldom getting out of debt until they go to the public works to get out. They settle on these farms, have large families generally, and simply crowd us out, causing us to seek a village or town where white people can co-operate, have schools and churches, and where it is understood that no Negroes own lots mixed with white people."

Poe therefore drops the subject of the wretched underpaid and ruthlessly exploited peonage and addresses himself to this dangerous newcomer:

"Briefly I should say that the law we need is one which will say that wherever the greater part of the land acreage in any given district that may be laid off is owned by one race, a majority of the voters in such a district may say (if they wish) that in future no land shall be sold to a person of a different race, provided such action is approved or allowed (as being justified by considerations of the peace, protection and social life of the community) by a reviewing judge or board of county commissioners."

He goes on to develop his thought: "Atlanta has just passed a law saying that a majority of property owners in a city block can say that in future no land shall be sold to a person of a different race from them. Why, then, cannot Georgia or any other State pass a law giving a similar privilege to its country people? Why can it not be said that where there is a white community and the majority of white land owners wish to keep their community white, they can layoff a district in which it will be unlawful to sell to a person of a different race? And since the same privilege would be given Negroes where they own land, the law could not

145

be said to discriminate against any race; and the whites would lose little because they do not care to buy in communities wholly surrounded by Negroes anyhow."

This has a certain semblance of even-handed justice. Mr. Poe says: "It may be argued, I know, that such a law is unjust, that with the government of the South as it is, it could be utilized by white people to keep their communities white, but the Negroes would rarely be able to use it to keep their communities wholly Negro. All of which I admit is possible, and yet, as I have said, I believe it is just."

Why would the Negro "rarely be able" to make a wholly Negro community? Because Negroes do not vote, cannot select county commissioners, and consequently could not drive out the whites. Nevertheless, Mr. Poe is not moved.

"Studying it with all possible desire for truth and justice, I repeat, therefore, I cannot see that it is right or just to say that because a white majority shall have the right to limit future land sales to their race, a Negro majority must everywhere have exactly the same privilege."

The difficulty is that Mr. Poe has his eye on the landlords of the black belt where a few land barons still drive their slaves with the lash. He wants to reassure them that no matter if the blacks outnumber them ten to one they are not to be disturbed in their reign.

But Mr. Poe's correspondents are not so canny. One of them says: "It is the gravest problem confronting us of the South to-day—this selling land promiscuously to the Negro race. In my neighborhood the white school population is twelve. The Negro school population is 140. Can I be satisfied to raise my children under such conditions? I am trying to sell out. Have been offered $12,000 cash for my farm by a Negro. It is worth $20,000 and would bring it if the surroundings were different."

At this we rub our eyes. If the Negro population outnumbers the white ten to one, surely this is the place, if any, for the white man to move. But this man does not want to move. What does he want there? Does he want the Negroes to go? No, but he wants them kept down. He does not even want to allow them the advantage of their disadvantages. As one says: "In protecting their home and social life, it is necessary for our rural white people to use some extraordinary measures to offset the Negroes' advantages in driving them out. In the first place, the Negro can live on less than the white man, and, therefore, if he is doing the same kind of work, he has this economic advantage over the white man."

Mr. Poe now appears in the offing again and serves this new argument: "It is Negro cheap labor that has ruined the South." "Why is Southern agriculture so far behind the North?" he asks.

The answer is easy. "The man in the North was driven to do his own work because he did not have scores of Negroes to do it, and this caused him to look around and seek other means with which to do it. And see how he has profited because he has always had to do his own labor, and see the great rut we now find ourselves in because we had plenty of Negroes to do our work, and therefore did not need to seek to improve our farm labor conditions as our Northern neighbor did."

The answer to this would seem obvious; make Negro labor dearer by turning it into an independent farm-owning class. But no, Mr. Poe will have none of this, but reports this case:

"I was reared and am now living in a community that only a few years ago was famed for its social features—live, well-filled churches and schools. But alas! it is hopelessly ruined. Churches and schools can hardly hold together. There are three non-resident land owners who are responsible for it all. This being a very fertile section, they have bought most of the land and want only Negro tenants. The land is unsurpassed for fertility by any section in several miles radius, and therefore has induced *the best type of Negroes* to cultivate it; *but, nevertheless, they are Negroes* and have completely destroyed the social features of the community." (The italics are ours.)

It would seem from this that there is no place on earth for the best Negroes either as tenants or land owners. Their very presence destroys all real life. "We might as well admit," says Mr. Poe, "the argument that the present wholesale sandwiching of whites and Negroes in our rural districts is perhaps the main thing in the way of developing rural co-operation in the South. If we can once get groups of wholly white communities, it will be far easier to get the farmers in them to pull together; whereas, at present, the white people in the South are too scattered to win success with 10,000 co-operative enterprises that would succeed if white farmers were grouped together. And especially does the present sandwiching of whites and Negroes militate against education—against good schools for both races."

But if educational justice is not done to the Negro in the white community, will it be done anywhere? One Negro correspondent is in despair. He writes: "If we own a good farm or horse or cow, dog or yoke of oxen, we are harassed until we are bound to sell, give away or run away before we can have any peace of our lives."

Mr. Poe prints this, but with apology and warning:

"We may say in this connection that it was our idea in printing the letters from Negroes simply to show what they are saying and thinking, and to give all sides a fair hearing. And if Negroes are bragging that they send their children to school when white people keep theirs away for lack of fine clothes, or because they are shut up in factories, or if they brag that there are white people who can't read and write, and they help them, or that white people won't work and the Negroes will, it will be a mighty good thing if we get mad enough about such boasting to see to it that they shall have no excuse even for saying such things in the future."

Mr. Poe, therefore, repeatedly returns to his original proposal. He has no fear of constitutions.

"It may be that the Atlanta segregation and the similar segregation plans we have suggested for our country districts might be declared in conflict with the Fourteenth Amendment. Some lawyers think so, some do not. But we report that if our people make up their minds that segregation is a good and necessary thing, they will find a way to put it into effect—just as they did in the case of Negro disfranchisement despite an iron-bound amendment specifically designed to prevent it.

"If such a direct law as we proposed last week would be unconstitutional, might not the same result be effected indirectly by saying that no land should be sold to any man in any specified district if a petition against the sale were signed by a majority of the resident land owners in such a district? If a predominantly white community, then it could be understood (or formally declared) that this new law would be invoked only to keep the community white, and so the matter would be settled without further trouble."

It is objected to by some that the plan does not go far enough. For example, the Knoxville (Tenn.) *Sentinel* says that "It seems to have a practical weakness, as so far advanced, that it does not take tenants into account."

"Well, there is no doubt that the indiscriminate renting of land to Negroes by absentee land owners is a crying evil. The letters we have received from all over the South indicate that unmistakably. And yet we do not now see any plan of regulating this evil that would not be susceptible of much abuse. As yet the proportion of white people wanting to rent land is small, and it would not be fair to absolutely limit the renting to white people even in these white communities.

"But it is our confident conviction that if the Negroes should refuse to work where the white people decided upon such a measure of protection, it would only be a form of industrial suicide fop there, and after a few months of trouble in working out a new adjustment, the white people would be as well off, or better off, from a labor standpoint than ever before. In the first place, young Southern white men would be willing to go into these all-white communities and work as laborers, and, in the second place, it would not be long until good white labor would come in from other sections."

Here, then, is the culmination of this extraordinary argument:

The South says here: We despise the Negro because he is down and yet we cannot allow him to rise; we cannot educate him lest he grow intelligent, we cannot allow him in industry lest he compete with us and save money; we cannot allow him to buy property because he will be independent and live beside us; we cannot let him live by himself because we want his labor, and because we dare not give him political power enough to establish and protect his own segregated communities.

The South is not wholly to blame for this logic. The North shares that blame. The high and only tenable ground of the past was: Educate the Negro, give him work and wages, give him civil rights, give him a vote and let him make his own way as a free man.

This ground the North has joined the South in undermining; they have half ruined his schools, they have curtailed his work and lowered his wages, they have made him a legal pariah and social outcast, and now they are coolly proposing to steal the bits of property which by the sweat of his face he has saved.

For stealing it is. Everybody knows that segregation is confiscation. Have we not the shameful treatment of the Indian to prove this?

How fine a program of solving the race problem this is which, after twenty-five years of trumpeting and advertising, lands us right in the same black slough of despond out of which we are just starting to raise the robbed and raped Indian. Fine statesmanship for the twentieth century—fine cowardice for the land of the free.

REVIEW OF THOMAS JESSE JONES' NEGRO EDUCATION (1918)[27]

The casual reader has greeted this study of Negro education with pleasure. It is the first attempt to cover the field of secondary and higher education among colored Americans with anything like completeness. It is published with the sanction and prestige of the United States government and has many excellent points as, for instance, full statistics on such matters as the public expenditure for Negro school systems, the amount of philanthropy given private schools, Negro property, etc; there is excellent and continued insistence upon the poor support which the colored public schools are receiving today. The need of continued philanthropic aid to private schools is emphasized and there are several good maps. Despite, then, some evidently careless proofreading (pages 59, 129, 157), the ordinary reader unacquainted with the tremendous ramifications of the Negro problem will hail this report with unstinted praise.

Thinking Negroes, however, and other persons who know the problem of educating the American Negro will regard the Jones report, despite its many praiseworthy features, as a dangerous and in many respects unfortunate publication.

---

27 Originally appeared in *The Crisis,* February 1918. Du Bois is reviewing Jones, Thomas Jesse. *Negro Education: A Study of the Private and Higher Schools for Colored People in the United States.* Washington, D.C.: Department of the Interior, 1916.

Thomas Jesse Jones (1873-1950) was an educator who spent much of his professional years working with and assessing education for African Americans in the generation following Emancipation. His adherence to principles of industrial education—practices championed most notably by Booker T. Washington—was so strong that recommendations for many of the schools cited in the report which did NOT adhere to those principles was that they be redesigned to reflect industrial education or that they be shuttered.

The Thesis of The Report

This report again and again insists by direct statements by inference and by continued repetition on three principles of a thesis which we may state as follows: *First,* that the present tendency toward academic and higher education among Negroes should be restricted and replaced by a larger insistence on manual training, industrial education, and agricultural training; *secondly,* the private schools in the South must "cooperate" with the Southern whites; and, *third;* that there should be more thoroughgoing unity of purpose among education boards and foundations working among Negroes.

The Negro College

The whole trend of Mr. Jones' study and of his general recommendations is to make the higher training of Negroes practically difficult, if not impossible, despite the fact that his statistics show (in 1914–15) only 1,643 colored students studying college subjects in all the private Negro schools out of 12,726 pupils. He shows that there are (in proportion to population) ten times as many whites in the public high schools as there are colored pupils and only sixty-four public high schools for Negroes in the whole South! He shows that even at present there are few Negro colleges and that they have no easy chance for survival. What he is criticizing, then, is not the fact that Negroes are tumbling into college in enormous numbers, but their wish to go to college and their endeavor to support and maintain even poor college departments.

What, in fact, is back of this wish? Is it merely a silly desire to study "Greek," as Mr. Jones several times intimates, or is it not rather a desire on the part of American Negroes to develop a class of thoroughly educated men according to modern standards?

152

If such a class is to be developed these Negro colleges must be planned as far as possible according to the standards of white colleges, otherwise colored students would be shut out of the best colleges of the country.

The curriculum offered at the colored southern colleges, however, brings the author's caustic criticism. Why, for instance, should "Greek and Latin" be maintained to the exclusion of economics, sociology, and "a strong course in biology?"

The reason for the maintenance of these older courses of study in the colored colleges is not at all, as the author assumes, that Negroes have a childish love for "classics." It is very easily and simply explicable. Take, for instance, Fisk University. Fisk University maintained Greek longer than most northern colleges, for the reason that it had in Adam K. Spence not simply a finished Greek scholar, pupil of the great D'Ooge, but a man of singularly strong personality and fine soul. It did not make much difference whether the students were studying Greek or biology—the great thing was that they were studying under Spence. So, in a large number of cases the curriculum of the southern Negro college has been determined by the personnel of the available men. These men were beyond price and working for their devotion to the cause. The college was unable to call men representing the newer sciences—young sociologists and biologists; they were unable to equip laboratories—but they did with infinite pains and often heartbreaking endeavor keep within touch of the standard set by the higher northern schools and the proof that they did well came from the men they turned out and not simply from the courses they studied.

This, Mr. Jones either forgets or does not know and is thus led into exceedingly unfortunate statements as when, for instance, he says that the underlying principle of the industrial school "is the adaptation of educational activities whether industrial or literary to the needs of the pupils and the community," which is, of course, the object of any educational institution and it is grossly unfair to speak of it as being the object of only a part of the great Negro schools of the South. Any school that does not have this for its object is not a school but a fraud.

The Public Schools

Not only does this report continually decry the Negro college and its curriculum but, on the other hand, it seeks to put in its place schools and courses of study which make it absolutely impossible for Negro students to be thoroughly trained according to modern standards. To illustrate: Mr. Jones shows (page 90) that in Butte, Mont., manual training has been put into the elementary schools at the rate of *half a day a week* during the first six years and *two half days a week* in the seventh and eighth grades. When, however, it comes to the smaller elementary industrial schools of the South Mr. Jones recommends *one-half day* classroom work and *one-half* practice in the field and shops *every day*.

What, now, is the real difference between these two schemes of education? The difference is that in the Butte schools for white pupils, a chance is held open for the pupil to go through high school and college and to advance at the rate which the modern curriculum demands; that in the colored schools, on the other hand, a program is being made out that will land the boy at the time he becomes self-conscious and aware of his own possibilities in an educational *impasse*. He cannot go on in the public schools even if he should move to a place where there are good public schools because he is too old. Even if he has done the elementary work in twice the time that a student is supposed to, it has been work of a kind that will not admit him to a northern high school. No matter, then, how gifted the boy may be, he is absolutely estopped from a higher education. This is not only unfair to the boy but it is grossly unfair to the Negro race.

The argument, then, against the kind of school that is being foisted upon Negroes in the name of industrial education is not any dislike on the part of the Negroes for having their children trained in vocations, or in having manual training used as a means of education; it is rather in having a series of schools established which deliberately shut the door of opportunity in the face of bright Negro students.

Industrial Training

With the drive that has been made to industrialize elementary schools before the children have learned to read and write and to turn the high schools to vocational teaching without giving any of the pupils a chance to train for college, it is, of course, beside the mark to criticize the colored colleges because the children that come to them are poorly trained.

Much of the criticism of colored teachers is also unfair. Even well-trained teachers are having curious pressure put upon them...

With its insistent criticizing of Negro colleges this report touches with curious hesitation and diffidence upon the shortcomings of industrial schools. Their failure to distinguish between general education, and technical trade training has resulted in sending out numbers of so-called teachers from educational schools who cannot read and write the English language and who are yet put in public and other schools as teachers. They may show children how to make tin pans and cobble shoes, but they are not the right persons to train youth, mentally or morally. In the second place, most of the trades taught by these trade schools are, because of hostile public opinion and poverty, decadent trades: carpentry, which is rapidly falling below the level of skilled trades; the patching of shoes; blacksmithing, in the sense of repair work, etc. The important trades of the world that are today assembled in factories and call for skilled technique and costly machinery are not taught in the vast majority of Negro industrial schools. Moreover, the higher industrial training calls for more education than the industrial schools give...

That the course of study in the southern schools as well as in the schools of the nation has got to be changed and adapted is absolutely true, but the object of a school system is to carry the child as far as possible in its knowledge of the accumulated wisdom of the world and then when economic or physical reasons demand that this education must stop, vocational training to prepare for life work should follow. That some of this vocational training may be made educational in object is true; that normal training may use manual training and even to some extent vocational training is true, but it is not true that the industrializing of any curriculum necessarily makes it better or that you can at one and the same time educate the race in modern civilization and train it simply to be servants and laborers. Anyone who suggests by sneering at books and "literary courses" that the great heritage of human thought ought to be displaced simply for the reason of teaching the technique of modern industry is pitifully wrong and, if the comparison must be made, more wrong than the man who would sacrifice modern technique to the heritage of ancient thought.

Cooperation

The second part of Mr. Jones' thesis lies in an insistence that the private schools of the Negro should "cooperate" with the South. He stresses the adaptation of education to the needs of the "community" (page 18), evidently meaning the *white* community. He quotes on page 25 the resolution of the white Southern Educational

Association which deplores that the Negro schools are isolated from the "community," meaning again the *white* community. He instances Willcox County, Ala., where there are almost no public schools and recommends that the private schools established there be put under "community" authorities (page 149). Now what is this "community" with which the colored people are to cooperate?

In the first place, Mr. Jones admits (pages 4 and 5), that it is only the progressive few in the white South that care anything at all about Negro schools. He might go even further and acknowledge that if a plebescite [sic] were taken tomorrow in the South the popular vote of white people would shut every single Negro school by a large majority. The hostile majority is kept from such radical action by the more progressive minority and by fear of northern interference, but the condition in which they have today left the colored schools is shown by this report to be truly lamentable.

Mr. Jones quotes from southern white men who speak of Negro school houses as "miserable beyond all description," of teachers as "absolutely untrained" and paid "the princely fortune of $80.92 for the whole term." He goes on with fact after fact to show the absolute inadequacy in the provision for colored children in the public schools of the South. On the other hand, he shows the increase in Negro property, the larger and larger amounts which Negroes are contributing to the school funds; and with all this he practically asks that the domination of the Negro private schools, which are now bearing the burden of nearly all the secondary and higher education of the Negro and much of the elementary education that the domination of these schools be put into the hands of the same people who are doing so little for the public schools!

There is not in the *whole* report a *single* word about *taxation without representation*. There is not a single protest against a public school system in which the public which it serves has absolutely no voice, vote, or influence. There is no defense of those colored people of vision who see the public schools being used as training schools for cheap labor and menial servants instead of for education and who are protesting against this by submitting to double taxation in the support of private schools; who cannot *see* that these schools should be turned over to people who by their actions prove themselves to be enemies of the Negro race and its advancement.

Until the southern Negro has a vote and representation on school boards public control of his education will mean his spiritual and economic death and that despite the good intentions of the small white minority in the South who believe in justice for the Negro. It is, therefore, contradictory for this report to insist, on the one hand, on the continuation of northern philanthropy for these schools and, on the other, to commend various southern schools in proportion as they have gained the approval of the white community.

Compare, for instance, Fisk University and Atlanta University. Both Cravath of Fisk and Ware of Atlanta were men radical in their belief in Negro possibility and in their determination to establish well equipped Negro colleges. Cravath, however, lived in a more enlightened community which was earlier converted to his ideals. He did not yield his opinion any more than Ware, but Ware lived in a community that to this day will not furnish even a high school for its colored pupils. To say that Fisk should receive on this account more support than Atlanta is rank injustice; if anything Atlanta deserves the greater credit.

Cooperation with the white South means in many cases the surrender of the very foundations of self-respect. Mr. Jones inserts in his report one picture of a colored principal and his assistant waiting on table while the white trustees of his school eat. The colored people of the South do not care a rap whether white folks eat with them or not, but if white officials are coming into their schools as persons in control or advisors, then to ask that in those schools and in their homes the colored people shall voluntarily treat themselves as inferiors is to ask more than any self-respecting man is going to do.

The white community, undoubtedly, wants to keep the Negro in the country as a peasant under working conditions least removed from slavery. The colored man wishes to escape from those conditions. Mr. Jones seeks to persuade him to stay there by asserting that the advance of the Negro in the rural South has been greatest (pages 97 and 123), and he refers to the "delusion" of city life even among white people. This may be all good enough propaganda but, in fact, it is untrue. Civilization has always depended upon the cities. The advance of the cities has been greatest for all people, white and colored, and for any colored-man to take his family to the country districts of South Georgia in order to grow and develop and secure education and uplift would be idiotic.

Mr. Jones touches the State schools very lightly. Here are cases where the whites have control and stories of graft and misappropriation of funds and poor organization are well known to everybody with the slightest knowledge of southern conditions. Teachers there and in the public schools are often selected not from the best available, but from the worst or most complacent. In small towns and country districts white trustees may maintain their mistresses as teachers and the protest of the colored people has fallen upon deaf ears. Until, then, colored people have a voice in the community, surrender to the domination of the white South is unthinkable.

Northern Philanthropy

This brings us to the third part of Mr. Jones' thesis, namely, that the boards working for southern education should unite as far as possible with one policy. This is an unfortunate and dangerous proposal for the simple reason that the great dominating philanthropic agency, the General Education Board, long ago surrendered to the white South by practically saying that the educational needs of the white South must be attended to before any attention should be paid to the education of Negroes; that the Negro must be trained according to the will of the white South and not as the Negro desires to be trained. It is this board that is spending more money today in helping Negroes learn how to can vegetables than in helping them to go through college. It is this board that by a system of interlocking directorates bids fair to dominate philanthropy toward the Negro in the United States. Indeed, the moving thought back of the present report is the idea of a single authority who is to say which Negro school is right or is wrong, which system is right and which is wrong, etc.

No one doubts the efficiency of concentration and unity in certain lines of work but always, even in work that can be unified, the question is *whose* influence is going to dominate; it may well be that diversity and even a certain chaos would be better than unity under a wrong idea. This is even more true in educational than in economic matters. Of course, the economic foundation of all recent educational philanthropy, particularly toward the Negro, is evident. Mr. Jones rather naively speaks of the fact that at certain times of the year "it is exceedingly difficult to prevail upon children to attend school" in the colored South which is, of course, another way of saying that bread and butter in the cotton fields is of more importance than trained intelligence.

Undoubtedly, there has already been a strong public opinion manufactured in the country which looks upon the training of Negroes in the South as cheap, contented labor to be used in emergency and for keeping white union labor from extravagant demands as a feasible and workable program. It is, in fact, one of the most dangerous programs ever thought out and is responsible for much of the lynching, unrest, and unhappiness in the South. Its genesis came easily with the idea of working *for* the Negro rather than working *with* him, a thing which Mr. Jones condemns, but hardly lives up to his condemnation.

In this very report the Negro was practically unrepresented. Instead of choosing a strong, experienced colored man to represent the Negro race (like W.T.B. Williams, or President Young of Tallahassee, or President Hope of Morehouse) an inexperienced young man was taken, of excellent character but absolutely without weight or influence. Of course, back of all this is the great difficulty of ordinary social intercourse. The reason that boards of trustees like those that control the Phelps Stokes Fund find it so much easier to work *for* the Negro than *with* him; the reason that forgetting the investigations by Negroes at Atlanta University they turned to white institutions to encourage investigation and neglected established and worthy work is because if they are going to cooperate with the dominant white South and even with certain classes of Northerners they cannot meet Negroes as men. The propaganda that is so largely carried on and the influence that is so often formed through social intercourse must always, at present, be offered with the Negro unrepresented and unheard.

There follows easily the habit of having no patience with the man who does not agree with the decisions of such boards. The Negro who comes with his hat in his hand and flatters and cajoles the philanthropist—that Negro gets money. If these foundations raise, as they do in this report, the cry of fraud they have themselves to thank. They more than any other agency have encouraged that kind of person. On the other hand, the Negro who shows the slightest independence of thought or character is apt to be read out of all possible influence not only by the white South but by the philanthropic North.

If philanthropic agencies could unite for certain obvious great movements how splendid it would be! Take, for instance, the duplication of higher educational schools which Mr. Jones repeatedly denounces and which, undoubtedly, is a source of weakness. The General Education Board could settle the matter with the greatest ease. Let it offer in Atlanta an endowment of $500,000 for a single Negro college, provided that there be but one college there for Negroes. The boards of the different schools immediately would have something to act upon. As it is, nothing that they can do individually would really better the situation. A new college formed by a federation of colored colleges in Atlanta, Marshall, Texas, and elsewhere, would be easily possible if an endowment was in sight.

Summary

Here, then, is the weakness and sinister danger of Mr. Jones' report. It calls for a union of philanthropic effort with no attempt to make sure of the proper and just lines along which this united effort should work. It calls for cooperation with the white South without insisting on the Negro being represented by voice and vote in such "cooperation," and it calls for a recasting of the educational program for Negroes without insisting on leaving the door of opportunity open for the development of a thoroughly trained class of leaders at the bottom, in the very beginnings of education, as well as at the top.

THE RULING PASSION (1922)[28]

Those years immediately following the Emancipation Proclamation startle one at times with their record of astounding achievement on the part of ex-slaves. It is only when we stop to realize that they represented the first outlet for centuries of the stifled desire and ambition of a thwarted people that we can understand how inevitably dynamic they hart to be, a sort of metamorphosis of time into action.

Men were single-minded in those days, possessing that attribute which is the first ingredient in the mixture of qualities that make for an individual success. It is easy to see how the black boy of 70 years ago was already beginning to say to himself, "If ever I am free, there's one thing I will do." And then when freedom unbelievably, amazingly came he said to himself again: "If Freedom were possible, all things are possible, I must let nothing stand in my way."

The star of achievement to which Joseph Price, a black boy of those days, hitched his wagon was the founding of a school for colored youth, a sort of black Harvard. It turned out in the course of his career that he was to be offered many prizes—a government position, a seat in the Liberian mission, a bishopric, but each of these he steadfastly refused in order to pursue his cherished dream, the establishment of Livingstone College at Salisbury, N.C.

These were remarkable prizes for those days, but Joseph Price would none of them. From the day on which in 1862 he entered

---

28 Originally appeared in *The Crisis*, March 1922.

Joseph Charles Price (1854–1893) was the founding president of Livingstone College in Salisbury, North Carolina. The two men expressed mutual admiration; Du Bois sought Price's counsel during his difficulties securing funding for study in Europe (see "Letter to Rutherford B. Hayes" dated May 25, 1891 in this volume). This article was written on the occasion of Price's 68th birthday anniversary.

the Sunday School in St. Andrew's Chapel in Newbern, N.C., his heart was fixed. He was 8 years old then, small and black and barefooted, of "stern but pleasant looks." That sternness of expression no doubt due to the singleness, the concentration of purpose which was even then beginning to show in his face.

From the beginning he himself must have felt that he was destined "to be somebody." Else why his eagerness to know all things? He beleaguered his teachers with questions. He answered those of other people. He had to have a mastery of wisdom for some day he meant to be a fountain himself for thirsty seekers after knowledge.

A good teacher makes a good pupil. As young as he was Price realized this for although in 1866 we find him a student in the St. Cyprian Episcopal School, by 1871 at the age of 17 he was teaching at Wilson. N. C. But being a teacher he learned his own limitations and back he went to school at Shaw University (already in action for those eager freedmen and their sons) and then on to Lincoln University at Oxford, Pa.

He had meanwhile become interested in religion and had connected himself with the A.M.E. Zion church. After the fashion of those days it seemed to him to be the thing; to combine pedagogy with theology so during his senior year in college he entered the junior theological department graduating thence in 1881.

It was while he was at Lincoln that Congressman John A. Hyman, of Newbern offered him a government position. The office paid $1.200 a year, a fortune in those days for a black man, but Joseph Price had the artist's sense of values, he knew what he wanted and that was not gold. He was like the poet preferring to mull over his precious verse, starving in an attic rather than opulently to finger the tape in a broker's office.

The gods had bestowed on him that not infrequent gift of his race, the art of persuasive oratory. He had already distinguished himself along this line in college. When he graduated in 1879 he was valedictorian. Before he came out of the theological school he was sent as a delegate to the A.M.E. Zion general conference in Montgomery and because of his gift he was ordained elder before even he had obtained his degree as a minister. After his graduation he was sent to the Ecumenical Conference which convened in London.

He directed the golden flow of his gift into one channel only, that of interesting people in the project of his school. At the close of the Ecumenical Conference he remained abroad to lecture in England, Scotland and Ireland. He returned with $10,000 with which in conjunction with another $1,000 given by the white merchants of Salisbury, he purchased the site of Livingstone College.

Of course he did other things and met with other honors. He became the acknowledged orator of his day, he was acclaimed a new leader, he was delegate at the Centenary of American Methodism in Baltimore in 1884. He was chairman of the A.M.E. and A.M.E. Zion Church Commission held in those days in Washington, D.C. He was president of the Afro-American League. Preparations were made for a Grand Southern Exposition and he was appointed Commissioner-General.

But the outstanding facts of his life are these. He was born in slavery and by the time he was 28 he had started a great school which 14 years after his death in 1893, at its quarto-centenary, had grown to astounding proportions. It had real estate valued at $250,000. In the course of its existence it had enrolled 6,500 pupils from 26 states. Its large faculty was comprised mainly of graduates from the collegiate, theological and normal departments. Among its alumni were numbered a bishop, presiding elders, well-known ministers, successful teachers and physicians, and all of these arose and called the name of Joseph Price blessed.

We Americans ascribe to Englishmen the quality of political diplomacy, to Frenchmen that of finesse and to ourselves the quality of grit. I like to think of Joseph Price, tall, majestic, superb of physique, of unmixed African blood as the epitome of his country's national characteristic.

DIUTURNI SILENTI (1924)[29]

From 1910 to 1924, I was out of direct touch with Negro education. There came the world of war during which I had sent my daughter to Bedales School in England, thinking the war would be short. She was forced to come home in 1914, and went to the Brooklyn Girls' High School. She did not like it. The teaching methods and the atmosphere were strange to her. She stuck it out and graduated, but was indifferent to a college course. It occurred to me that she might be as thrilled as I once was, if she went south to Fisk. I applied for admission after she was graduated from high school and there was some rather curious and to me inexplicable hesitation, but she was finally admitted. She seemed happy there. She made no complaints. Yet there filtered through certain criticisms of the Fisk of 1924, and once when I was visiting there a student came to me, slipping up almost furtively in the twilight.

It was my first talk with George Streator, then a junior. He said to me: "Don't you want to know what is going on at Fisk?" Afterward I opened my ears. I listened, wrote and investigated, and I was astonished at a state of affairs of which I had not dreamed. When I complained to my daughter for not telling me of conditions, she answered placidly: "I thought you knew!" The student discipline at Fisk had retrograded so as to resemble in some respects a reform school. The administration of the school seemed based on organized gossip. The desperate attempt to get funds had led to a surrender to Southern sentiment compared to which the overtures of Dr. Merrill were but faint and unimportant. The spirit of the school seemed

---

29   Title translated, "The Long Silence." From Cicero's "For Marcellus." Translation by C.D. Yonge, (1891).

Transcript of a speech given in February, 1924 on the campus of Fisk University, Nashville, Tennessee. A transcript of the speech was reprinted in the *Fisk Herald*, in April of 1924.

wrong and from time to time teachers, students, and graduates appealed to me.

Again it was the date of one of my continually reoccurring reunions. In 1923, I had been graduated thirty-five years. I had not spoken that year because my daughter was graduating the next year; and so in 1924 I came to Fisk University determined to do an unpleasant duty and do it thoroughly. I determined to voice the widespread criticism of alumni, students, and friends of Fisk University at the way in which the president, trustees, and faculty were conducting the school and I was going to do it at Fisk, face to face with its officials. And so in the Memorial Chapel with my back to the great organ and with the president and his wife sitting in front of me and the alumni ranged row on row, while the undergraduates looked down from the gallery in suspense, I literally "lifted my voice and taught them saying:"

> *Diuturni silenti, patres conscripti, quo eram his temporibus usus—non timore aliquo, sed partim dolore, partim verecundia—finem hodiernus dies attulit, idemque initium quae vellem quaeque sentirem meo pristino more dicendi.*

You who have not wholly forgotten your Latin, will remember that the two words of my subject are taken from the beginning of Cicero's oration in defense of Marcellus. I recall the stilted translation thereof which I committed to memory in my boyhood:

> *To my long continued silence, Conscript Fathers, which I have made use of in these days, not on account of any fear, but partly from grief, partly from shame, this day brings an end and also a beginning of my speaking according to my former custom what I think and what I know.*

To make these perhaps somewhat cryptic words more clear to you, may I say a few words concerning my connection with Fisk University. I was graduated from Fisk thirty-six years ago this month after three years of splendid inspiration and nearly perfect happiness, under teachers whom I respected and amid surroundings that inspired me. I regarded the ten years after my graduation from 1888 to 1898 simply as a sort of prolongation of my Fisk college days. I was at Harvard but not of it. I was a student of Berlin, but still the son of Fisk; and I came back to Fisk to deliver the commencement address in 1898 and to make that address a welcome to my younger fellows into the high calling of those who had gone forth from this institution with fine determination and splendid inspiration.

Ten other years passed and when I returned here as alumni speaker in 1908, there was a shadow as it seemed to me already across this institution. The trend toward industrial education was to my mind beginning to lower the standards and vitiate the ideals for higher college training which were the heritage of Fisk University. I spoke my complaint clearly and sought to warn this institution that it would never do, for purposes of expediency, to lie to the world as Galileo once lied when he knew that his heart held the truth. This speech of mine was received with much criticism, and from that time to this, sixteen years, I have not been invited to speak at this institution. Once or twice when I happened of necessity to be on the grounds I have been invited to say a few

Video Sidebar

Westbrook tells the story of "The Long Silence" and Du Bois' frustration with the Black community for not using their knowledge to raise their race.

http://youtu.be/n010-CP_LvA

words and have made perfunctory remarks knowing that nothing further was expected. I knew too that my thoughts and ideals were distasteful to those from whom Fisk at this time was expecting financial aid, and as I had neither money nor monied friends I took refuge in silence even when I sensed wrong.

Today I recognize that my invitation to address the alumni is largely a matter of circumstances and not of deliberate choice on the part of this institution. Nevertheless I have come to address you and, I say frankly, I have come to criticize. I have known and been connected more or less intimately with many colored institutions of learning, but I have never known an institution whose alumni on the whole are more bitter and disgusted with the present situation in this university than the alumni of Fisk University today. This, of course, is not true of all the alumni, but it is true of so great and so important a part that Fisk University ought to know it.

I have come therefore to criticize and to say openly and before your face what so many of your graduates are saying secretly and behind your back. I maintain that the place to criticize Fisk University is at Fisk University and not elsewhere; and above all I maintain that this is the time and the critical time in the history of this institution when the opinion of its alumni and constituents must be known and decision must be taken by the trustees and faculty as to the future policy of Fisk University. And it is for this reason that I say: "To my long continued silence, Conscript Fathers, which I have made use of in these days, not on account of any fear, but partly from grief, partly from shame, this day brings an end and also a beginning of my speaking according to my former custom, what I think and what I know."

I come to defend two theses, and the *first* is this: *Of all the essentials that make an institution of learning, money is the least.* The *second* is this: *The alumni of Fisk University are and or right ought to be, the ultimate source of authority in the policy and government of this institution.*

Taking up the first thesis I do not, of course, mean for a moment to be so foolish as to say that a university does not need money. Fisk University does need money; any institution needs today physical equipment, buildings, laboratories, and salaries and needs them imperatively; and yet I do maintain that this equipment is not the greater need. I maintain that there is a spiritual equipment, without which no institution can really exist as a center of culture, and I trust that it will never be necessary to say of Fisk University as was once said of Brown University:

"Yesterday Brown University had a president; today it has a million dollars."

Three great things are necessary for the spiritual equipment of an institution of learning: *Freedom of Spirit, Self-Knowledge*, and a recognition of the *Truth*. These are trite phrases, but they are none-the-less eternally true; and *first* of all comes Freedom of Spirit.

It is a beautiful figure that we continually use in depicting the relationship of college and student; Alma Mater—Fostering Mother. We see always in this true relationship the arm of this old mother about the shoulders of her sons and grandsons and grandsons' grandsons, whispering to their ears. "Behold the beautiful land which the Lord thy God has given thee!" And nowhere is this inspiration needed more than in the case of colored students today. They come out of the Valley of the Shadow with souls that have been hurt and crushed, and the great duty of the Negro college is to say to these students that the little sordid things of earth and of ordinary life where they lack so much freedom, are as nothing compared with the great free realm of the spirit.

I have often told audiences of my experience when I went first to see the Bernese Oberland. I stood on the plaza of the cathedral at Berne and looked upon the Alps. I saw the great green hills and rising mountains. They were fine and I was glad. I started to turn away, and then, almost by accident, I lifted my eyes up to the sky, and there, above the hills and above the mountains, up where I had thought of nothing but mists and clouds, blazed in unearthly splendor the snow-capped Alps—sublime, magnificent. And so it is with these colored students. It is inspiration and light and the free, untrammeled spirit that rises above the earth which they seek in college. Through this very freedom comes discipline, and through discipline comes freedom.

What now is Fisk University doing to uphold and to spread the spirit of freedom in this institution? It is not doing what it should. In Fisk today, discipline is choking freedom; threats are replacing inspiration, iron-clad rules, suspicion, tale bearing are almost universal. A favorite expression is, "If you don't like Fisk University, get out!" If you do not agree with all the policies of the institution, go elsewhere. Students are made to promise in writing not simply to obey the rules of the institution but to obey *all future rules that maybe made.* Even during my short stay of a few days, I have seen crass instances of discipline. At the senior chapel, the last, and as it should have been, holiest exercise, everything was held up for five minutes until the presiding official publicly disciplined a few "giggling girls."

Instances of discipline have occurred here, almost criminal in their miscarriage of justice.

I have known a girl to be sent home for theft because she could not satisfactorily explain her possession of a five-dollar bill; and when afterward it was proven beyond a doubt that the money was rightfully hers, no apology was ever made. She was simply told quietly that she could come back. She has since graduated with honor at Howard University. To illustrate in what glaring contrast the present discipline of Fisk University stands with the discipline of my day let me recall one instance.

I was seventeen years old. Perhaps my older class mates were having fun at my expense, but at any rate I was told that at commencement time the ordinary rules did not hold. I consequently walked boldly up through yonder white gates and invited Dickey to take a walk. (She was called Dickey because her father wanted a son and named her Richard anyway.) We sauntered out the front gate in broad day light, down the long path, past Livingston, called at the city home of one of our fellow students, Lizzie Jones, found other students there and danced and ate. Then we walked back in the dying day and came to Jubilee Hall about sunset.

It looked as though the roof of the hall was about to rise. The matron was furious. "But I didn't know that I was breaking any rule," I stammered. I was given to understand that I ought to have known, which did not seem to me a bit logical; and then I came before the president. He was a tall, white-haired man with bushy eyebrows and deep eyes, in the depths whereof always lurked a smile. And he said to me quietly, "don't do it again." And I didn't. He bound me to him for time and eternity by that one wise judgment. He knew perfectly-well that if a boy is up to a nasty trick he doesn't walk out of the front gate in full daylight.

I do not for a moment doubt that the objects which Fisk today wishes to gain by her discipline are in themselves perfectly good objects; but the trouble is that she is trying to accomplish her ends by methods which are medieval, and long since discredited. The second and third generation of colored students present their problems of discipline and guidance, but those problems in the long run are no greater than the problems presented everywhere in the training of youth throughout the colleges of the United States and the world; and of all ways of treating these problems and settling them, the method of piling rule on rule and threat on threat is the worst and most ineffective, and it makes not men but hypocrites.

Fisk University wishes to be recognized by the great institutions of learning, and yet at other institutions students are being taught discipline through freedom. When Bertrand Russell was not allowed to speak at Harvard University the students protested not simply to the faculty but to the overseers, and their right to protest was freely recognized. No protest would for a moment be tolerated on the part of the students of Fisk. If a student even feels disagreement with the policies of Fisk he is given to understand that he is not wanted. It is the spirit of freedom that has built the great universities of the world, and Fisk can never be great until it recognizes that spirit. The pall of fear which envelops the student body of this institution is the most awful thing here.

The second great thing that characterizes an institution of learning is *Self-Knowledge*, the principle ancient as Greece and older: "Know Thyself." The students are in college for purposes of self-expression and experiment; to test their own wings, to find ability and strengthen character, to learn self-control. In such self-experience on the part of the young there is a cost to pay, a certain waste that is inevitable; the appearance of youthful swagger and impudence; and yet the wiser world has learned that in youth, even as in age, the Cost of Freedom is less than the Price of Repression. At Fisk University the temptation and the tendency is to cramp self-expression, reduce experiment to the lowest terms and cast everything in an iron mould. College women are put in uniforms in a day when we reserve uniforms for those who are organized to murder, for lackeys and for insane asylums and jails. Not only is the system of uniforms at Fisk ineffective and wasteful, but its method of enforcement is humiliating and silly.

The students are allowed to do almost nothing of their own initiative. They can have no organizations except such as are not simply supervised by the faculty but are in part run by the faculty with membership determined by the faculty, with some long-eared member of the faculty sitting in at every meeting to listen.

There can be no opinion expressed by the students in any public way. If I have any knowledge of the English language and any facility in expression that began with the three years spent on the editorial staff of the *Fisk Herald*. The *Fisk Herald* was for a long time one of the oldest student papers in the United States. It was a shame to suppress it. Other colored institutions even below college grade and practically all white institutions have their student papers. Fisk University is not allowed to have one. Athletics are hampered and threatened with extinction by faculty action.

Thus self-expression and manhood are choked at Fisk in the very day when we need expression to develop manhood in the colored race. We are facing a serious and difficult situation. We need every bit of brains and ability that we have for leadership. There is no hope that the American Negro is going to develop as a docile animal. He is going to be a man, and he needs therefore his best manhood. This manhood is being discouraged at Fisk today and ambition instead of being fostered is being deliberately frowned upon.

I met a young man the other day in an institution far from here. He walked up and stuck out his hand and said, "I am Hunter's son." I remembered Hunter in my college days at Fisk—a big, strong, muscular black man. He got angry once at some of my pert criticism and gripped me. I thought my arm was coming off. These were the days before the legal "Jim Crow" law, but the brakemen used to take it upon themselves to force all colored passengers into the smoking car. Hunter went down with the other students after commencement to board the train. The brakeman barred the way to the passenger coach. Hunter swept the brakeman aside with one arm and with the other beckoned the students. They walked into the coach singing. This was Hunter's son. I looked at him with interest. Why wasn't he at Fisk University? Is Fisk University afraid of men of this sort? Is this the kind of person that she expels for impudence? Is Fisk trying to make the roll of her expulsions a sort of roll of honor? Is she afraid to have these students know themselves?

The third thing that a university stands for is the recognition of *Truth*, the search for Truth. We say this glibly now, but we must remember that in every age while institutions of learning have accepted and taught certain parts of the truth there are other parts about which they have hesitated. For a long time geology could not be taught in our institutions because it interfered with the biblical "six days." Today some people are trying to enjoin the teaching of Evolution; and continually in our day the teaching of the truth concerning our social structure and economic development is being hindered and suppressed. That this is dangerous goes without saying; but the greatest of dangers faces those institutions of the South, white and colored, that are afraid to tell the truth concerning the difficult social environment in which the youth of the South is growing up.

One can imagine, of course, two extreme attitudes which a Negro college might take with regard to the surrounding South; it might teach that the case is hopeless; that no Negro can expect to be a man in this country with the present attitude and determination of the whites. Or it might go to the opposite extreme and say that all is well; that the best thought of the country is tending toward justice and that the Negro's only hindrance is himself. Neither of these positions is tenable. And a real university with honest purpose today ought frankly to face the fact that there are here forces of advancement and uplift, that there are forces of evil and retrogression, and that it is for the educated man to find a way amid these difficulties.

Fisk University is not taking an honest position with regard to the Southern situation. It has deliberately embraced a propaganda which discredits all of the hard work which the forward-looking fighters for Negro freedom have been doing. It over-praises the liberal white South. It continually teaches its students and constituency that this liberal white South is in the ascendency and that it is ruling; and that the only thing required of the black man is acquiescence and submission. Thus the *Fisk News*, speaking without right and without warrant for Fisk University, for its alumni and its constituency, is advocating and spreading a doctrine which every student in this university knows is dishonest. They know and they appreciate the things which the white friends of humanity living in the South are doing, but they know that these liberal white folk are not triumphant, that they are facing a terrific wall of prejudice and evil; and every day these students in their lives are experiencing this evil. They know "Jim Crow" cars; they know the effects of disfranchisement; they know personal and persistent insult. You cannot teach these children honesty as long as you dishonestly deny these truths which they know all too well.

Let me bring two things to your mind—and I am speaking now not of lawless lynchings and of the mob, but of the acts of Southern white men of the better class. There was a man in south Georgia, a colored man, upon whose land I once stood. He owned ten thousand acres free of debt. He had schools and churches, white tenants and colored tenants. The other day he died without a will and at the request of his inexperienced widow, his friend, the white banker, undertook to settle his estate. In less than a year every cent of this man's property was gone and today his girls are dancing in a cabaret in New York to support themselves and the widowed mother.

Or, to take another phase: In Birmingham, Alabama, the condition of the colored schools has long been a shame. At last in order to get a large bond issue of three million dollars, the best white citizens solemnly promised to spend five hundred thousand dollars upon the Negro schools. They proposed to put up a Negro high school to cost three or four hundred thousand dollars and one large primary school. They had, however, as principal of the colored high school a Negro tool and lickspittle. He assured them that the colored people didn't need any school as costly as they proposed. He asked for a straggling one-story building with a little brick and a great deal of stucco and at a cost of about half what they had proposed to spend. He achieved a partly finished high school. It is precisely such lickspittles and cowards that the propaganda carried on by the Fisk News is developing, and it will never be successful because it holds within itself its own contradiction and denial.

The truth concerning the present racial situation is systematically kept from Fisk students as well as the truth concerning the great liberal movements of the world. Representatives of the International Youth Movement complained that Fisk was one of the few American institutions where they were not allowed contact with the students. Representatives of colored fraternities with their "Go to High School, Go to College" campaign were not allowed to speak at Fisk. The National Association for the Advancement of Colored People, which has done more than any organization for the freedom of the Negro race and for making the interracial movement possible, has never been represented at Fisk University. And yet Fisk University pretends to be an institution for the presentation of the truth.

To recapitulate, Fisk University is choking freedom. Self-knowledge is being hindered by refusal of all initiative to the students. Fisk University is not teaching the truth about the race problem.

What is the reason for this state of affairs at Fisk? We colored people, talking among ourselves of the action of white folk toward us continually bring in one general essential cause and that is total depravity—the determination on the part of the white world to do us all possible ill.

Such a reason is, of course, fanciful in nearly all cases, and in this case I do not believe that those in control of Fisk University wish or desire anything but the welfare of the colored race. But the difficulty is that they do not know what is for our good or what we think is for our good. They have not before them facts that are well known to us and points of view and considerations which are to us of tremendous importance. It is in this case, as in so many others, ignorance that leads to evil.

Have you ever seen a king "By the grace of God?" I have. I remember as a young man walking down the *Unter den Linden* from the Royal Palace past the university and toward the Brandenburg Gate. Suddenly there would be a signal and the crowd would turn to the curb and stiffen, standing at attention. Far up the broad avenue came the flash of cream and silver, the waving of plumes; and the prancing of horses; and then he flew by, erect, stern and splendid, "*Wilhelm, von Gottes Gnade, Koenig von Preussen, Deutscher Kaiser.*" He has passed today. He was not a bad man, he was a mistaken one. He did not know. He did not call the real German people to council, and he failed because he did not know. And so whenever a man or a group of men assume to rule over others who are separated from them by class or racial or economic interest they are going to make terrible mistakes if the ruled and the rulers do not sit down and take counsel together. The theory of democracy is not that the people have all wisdom or all ability, but it is that the mass of people form a great reservoir of knowledge and information which the state will ignore at its peril.

So in Fisk University, there are at the service of the Trustees, the President, and the Faculty great streams of knowledge and experience; the knowledge and experience of these students here; the knowledge and experience of the whole black world in America which is more and more becoming bound together in organized unity. Fisk University is systematically ignoring these sources of information. It is not consulting the students, it is ordering them about. In only one of the commencement exercises that I have seen did the students have any chance to speak or express themselves, and in that case the President and Faculty were conspicuous by their absence, while the speeches were evidently carefully censored.

In the business which I conduct I payout over fifty thousand dollars a year; and yet in the fifteen years that I have conducted that business I have never been so threatened with penalties for debt as I have in the last four years in trying to pay my daughter's expenses at Fisk. It was almost impossible, in the first place, to find what sums were due and when they were to be paid; and when finally I did get notice it was almost invariably too late for me to forward a check before the date on which some penalty for nonpayment was due. Several times I have telegraphed funds. And I know of one father, one of the wealthiest graduates of Fisk whose daughter was publicly denied the right to get books at the book store while across the road at the treasury there lay a balance to her credit. Parents who try to get into sympathetic touch with this institution find no encouragement and those who visit it are usually treated with the scantest courtesy.

The alumni have no voice in the policy or conduct of the institution. They get no communications except a demand for contributions. Almost nothing is done to encourage alumni reunions. No careful record is kept of alumni activities, and while from time to time one or even two alumni are upon the Board of Trustees, they are alumni selected by the President and the Trustees and not by the Alumni Association; and they may or may not represent the opinion of the alumni.

The colored world of Nashville is entirely out of sympathy and out of touch with Fisk University. They attend the exercises held in dwindling numbers. I was present this year at one of the Mozart Society concerts. It was a fine exercise, with excellent singing and some of the greatest colored soloists in America, including Florence Cole Talbert. But the society sang to empty benches. I doubt if there were two hundred people in the chapel. And yet I have known the day when a young black boy from west Tennessee, almost untrained, sang that incomparable tenor solo from *The Messiah*, "Comfort ye, comfort ye, my People," to an audience that covered every inch of the old chapel in Livingston Hall. Today even at the exercises of commencement week there is plenty of room for everybody and sometimes wide empty spaces. The black world of Nashville, and not simply the educated, but the ordinary colored people, know that Fisk University does not want them; that it is straining every effort to attract Southern white people and is segregating and insulting its colored auditors.

Suppose that instead of this attitude the authorities of Fisk University took the trouble to consult their alumni and their constituents and their students. Take, for instance, the matter of clothes. There was once a colored leader who sneered at the pianos in the homes of poor colored people, but it was pointed out to his quick discomfiture that it was a fine thing for the poor to spend on music even that which they might have spent on bread. Did it not show the innate beauty of their souls? And so today Fisk University sneers and raves and passes all sorts of rules against the overdressing of its students, particularly of its women; and there is no doubt but what colored people of the better class waste money in personal adornment. At the same time consider for a moment the reasons: Have you ever ridden on a "Jim Crow" car? I have. I have just come here from riding on many. For the most part they are dirty, ugly, unpleasant. Have you ever been in the colored section of a Southern city? Despite the effort of the colored people to beautify their homes, the city leaves this section as muddy and nasty and unkempt and unprotected as possible. I just looked upon a new graded school in Atlanta. It was the ugliest building I have ever seen. It went out of its way to be ugly. I thought at first it was a factory of the meaner sort.

All through the life of colored people and of their children the world makes repeated efforts to surround them with ugliness. Is it a wonder that they flame in their clothing? That they desire to fill their starved souls with overuse of silk and color? They may fail in their object or overdo it, but now and then they do achieve startlingly fine results. I saw upon the campus this afternoon two girls. (Do not worry, they were not from Fisk University and did not break your rules.) They were dressed in filmy garments with scarfs of crimson and blue about their necks and the setting sun beyond Jubilee Hall threw its glory over them. They were a startlingly beautiful sight. I do not for a moment dispute that the parents of the girls of Fisk University tend to waste money on their clothes; but I do say that New England old maids dressed like formless frumps in dun and drab garments, have no right utterly to suppress and insult these children of the sun even if they want to wear silk; and that to inculcate good taste in dress is a far more subtle matter than stiff rules and harsh judgments.

Consider the matter of fraternities. Fisk University is the only one of the larger colored colleges which does not allow fraternities. There are many sound reasons of this attitude. We know what fraternities have done in the matter of snobbishness and disintegration in many of our large institutions. On the other hand, those institutions have not abolished fraternities and they must have their reasons. Moreover in the case of the colored fraternities their whole inner spirit and the reason for their being differentiates them entirely from white college organizations. They grew up in white northern colleges where colored students were suffering a social ostracism which interfered seriously with their college work. They spread to colored colleges because of the serious efforts which they were making to increase and vivify the college spirit. The "Go to High School, Go to College" campaign carried on annually by the Alpha Phi Alpha fraternity has been one of the greatest incentives in America to push colored youth toward higher education.

Not only is that fraternity not allowed in Fisk University, but its representatives could not even come there to speak on the higher education campaign. Another colored fraternity has its "Guide Right" campaign seeking to guide colored graduates into proper employment. The sororities are offering scholarships and prizes to colored graduates. Fisk University has no right autocratically and without consultation with or listening to the advice of students, parents, and alumni to ban these powerful and influential organizations and cut their graduates off from the best fellowship for life.

In northern Ohio there is the city of Cleveland. For fifty years the colored group in Cleveland has fought for municipal recognition and equality and it has accomplished a splendid work. Our great colored author, Charles W. Chesnutt, is a member of one of the leading literary and social clubs. A colored lawyer, Harry Davis, is a member of the Cleveland City Club and long has served in the Ohio Legislature. We have colored councilmen. We have colored teachers in the public schools who teach without segregation or discrimination. There is not a single "Jim Crow" institution in the city, and this is because with fifty years' fighting we have achieved real democracy in Cleveland.

Last year, Fisk University went to Cleveland and arranged a dinner and meeting with influential citizens, at which the President of the Board of Trustees and the President of the University spoke. No colored people were invited or expected. No colored people were consulted as to what ought to be said in that city. The next day the papers reported that Fisk University believed in segregation for colored people and thought it was inevitable and permanent! I am aware that explanations were made afterwards; that the speakers affirmed that they were expressing a fact and not a theory; but the best that can be said of them is that they awkwardly and maladroitly made statements that hurt the cause of the Negro in Cleveland and did the cause of Fisk no good. Suppose that before they staged this meeting they had had a little private talk with their alumni in Cleveland; or with Mr. Chesnutt or with Mr. Davis? They could have accomplished everything that they wanted to accomplish in this great and generous city and at the same time avoided affronting and discrediting a brave and struggling group.

How different it is in other institutions and in those very institutions with which it is the ambition of Fisk University to be recognized as of equal standing in scholarship! The president and authorities of Harvard University made up their minds to ban the Negro and the Jew; but when protest came from the alumni and the public they did not ignore it; they even encouraged it. They listened to it and they followed it, and they gave up a public policy which was as extraordinary as it was wrong.

The whole policy of segregation as it is developed at Fisk University is a menace and a disgrace. I am told that this year the Jubilee Club gave a concert downtown. Not only was the colored audience "Jim-Crowed" and segregated but the colored teachers were separated from the white teachers and different windows were furnished where colored and white people were to buy their tickets! When Isaiah Scott, a bishop of the Methodist Episcopal Church, went innocently to the white window, he was refused service and insulted. I am told that the President of Fisk University took fifteen or twenty girls from the Glee Club, girls from some of the best Negro families in the United States, carried them downtown at night to a white men's club, took them down an alley and admitted them through the servants' entrance and had them sing in a basement to Southern white men, while these men smoked and laughed and talked. If Erastus Cravath, the first president of this institution, knew that a thing like that had happened at Fisk University he would, if it were in any way possible, rise from the grave and protest against this disgrace and sacrilege.

I have said that these things are taking place at Fisk University mainly through ignorance, mainly because the present workers of this institution do not realize what they are doing or why they should not do these things. But there is, I confess, one other reason, a reason so sinister and so unfortunate that I hesitate to mention it; it is this: For a long time a powerful section of the white South has offered to give its consent and countenance to the higher training of Negroes only on condition that the white South control and guide that education. And it is possible that for a million dollars the authorities of Fisk University have been asked either openly or by implication to sell to the white South the control of this institution. It is not the first time that a Corrupt Bargain of this kind has been attempted. Its earlier form at Hampton and Tuskegee included an understanding that these institutions were not to do college work and that they were to furnish servants for white people.

Sincere and long continued attempts were made to carry out this program and they failed. Hampton has become a college and is increasing its college curriculum. The graduates of Tuskegee are not servants for white people and never will be. They are entering college and the professions in larger and larger numbers. Now comes the suspicion of a similar attempt at Fisk. Pressure has been put upon Fisk graduates to go into Southern domestic service, that branch of human activity which is, as the world knows, the chief source of prostitution and the degradation of human independence. If any such bargain as I have outlined has been consciously or unconsciously, openly or secretly entered into by Fisk University, I would rather see every stone of its buildings leveled and every bit of its activity stopped before the Negro race consents.

Back, of course, of suggestions and bargains like this lies the doctrine of the inferiority of the Negro race, and I shall never believe that an institution once taught and guided by men like Cravath and Spence and Chase can ever for a moment take a stand which does not regard the black race as an equal of any other race on earth.

This brings me to the second of the two theses which I outlined, namely, that *the alumni of Fisk University are and of right ought to be the ultimate source of authority in the policy and government of this institution.* The duty of rescuing Fisk rests upon us as graduates. It is a duty we may not shirk and before which we cannot longer hesitate. I know the thing that leaps to the minds of all of us. We are aware that every great institution in this land is conducted in the last analysis by its alumni, but we echo in our own case the criticism that is so often flung at us, namely, that we have not supported this institution, that very little of this new million dollar endowment has come from us.

I resent this criticism. The students of Fisk University pay as large a proportion of their expenses as the students of Harvard or other great Northern institutions. The money which their parents have given to Fisk University and to other public purposes forms a greater proportion of their income and a more costly amount of personal sacrifice than any money that any white group has given or ever will give to this institution. It is recognized the world over today that institutions of learning are the property of the community; that the community ought to support them and that the money given for that support, either given from the public treasury or from private sources, is not a dole to beggars but a debt to society. I resent, therefore, with every ounce of my energy, the sneer that the graduates of Fisk University are beggars with no right to rule this institution simply because they are for the most part men who have struggled and toiled and done their duty for low wages and little incomes, amid mob law and prejudice:

> If blood be the price of admiralty,—
> If blood be the price of admiralty,—
> If blood be the price of admiralty,—
> Lord God, we have paid in full![30]

Our duty is clear before us and our right to perform that duty. The steps that we should take include, *first, Publicity.* We must let the whole world know just what is happening at Fisk University. *Secondly, Organization;* instead of the loose, ineffective Alumni Association, the alumni and friends of this institution must be firmly knit together to rescue *Alma Mater. Thirdly,* we must demand elective representation on the Board of Trustees, beginning with one or two members and gradually as the years go on increasing until in another generation we shall control the Board.

Finally, while we are taking these steps and as long as present conditions at Fisk University continue, we must actively support

---

30   From Rudyard Kipling's "Song of the Dead," 1893.

by our advice the boycott of this institution which has already begun. The student body at Fisk is beginning to dwindle, and the dwindling has begun with the men because the men have more economic independence than the girls. Livingston Hall houses today about one-half the number of men students which it should house. Other schools are graduating dozens of students who either began their work at Fisk University or would have been glad to go there if they could have expected to be treated as men and women. And unless that treatment is forthcoming we must not encourage colored students to go there.

I know just what this means to us of sacrifice. We love Fisk. We are its children. We believe eternally in its undying spirit; but we cannot sacrifice the ideals of the Negro race and the democracy of the world to our personal selfishness. The Negro race needs colleges. We need them today as never before; but we do not need colleges so much that we can sacrifice the manhood and womanhood of our children to the Thoughtlessness of the North or the Prejudice of the South. Ultimately Fisk will and must survive. The spirit of its great founders will renew itself, and it is that Spirit alone, reborn, which calls us tonight.

Oh, be swift my soul, to answer Him, be jubilant my feet!
Our God is marching on! [31]

---

31 Postscript to the speech. While it was hailed by students and many Alumni, it was looked upon unfavorably by the Trustees and benefactors of Fisk. Notable among the detractors was Mrs. Margaret Murray Washington, widow of Booker T. Washington, and Fisk schoolmate of Du Bois. Always a fan of "young Willy," as she referred to him in years past, Murray Washington believed that Du Bois' incendiary speech might result in a loss of funding for the university. Despite not budging on their refusal to consider hiring a black president for another twenty years, most of the other demands made by the students were met. Shortly after delivering this speech, students at other "flagship" historically Black colleges such as Hampton, Lincoln and Howard found inspiration in Du Bois' speech and led similar protests against their respective administrations.

DOES THE NEGRO NEED SEPARATE SCHOOLS? (1935)[32]

There are in the United States some four million Negroes of school age, of whom two million are in school, and of these, four-fifths are taught by forty-eight thousand Negro teachers in separate schools. Less than a half million are in mixed schools in the North, where they are taught almost exclusively by white teachers. Beside this, there are seventy-nine Negro universities and colleges with one thousand colored teachers, beside a number of private secondary schools.

The question which I am discussing is: Are these separate schools and institutions needed? And the answer, to my mind, is perfectly clear. They are needed just so far as they are necessary for the proper education of the Negro race. The proper education of any people includes sympathetic touch between teacher and pupil; knowledge on the part of the teacher, not simply of the individual taught, but of his surroundings and background, and the history of his class and group; such contact between pupils, and between teacher and pupil, on the basis of perfect social equality, as will increase this sympathy and knowledge; facilities for education in equipment and housing, and the promotion of such extra-curricular activities as will tend to induct the child into life.

---

32   W.E.B. Du Bois. (July, 1935) "Does the Negro need separate schools?" *Journal of Negro Education, 4,* 328-335. Reprinted by permission of Howard University.

This article written nearly twenty years before the ground breaking *Brown v. Board of Education* Supreme Court decision was met with disapproval by the NAACP, which was in the midst of a contentious battle in the courts against school segregation. Despite the fact that Du Bois did not decry integration— he called "good schools," irrespective of racial makeup—it was feared that his words might be misconstrued as supporting segregation. Du Bois, aware of the potential backlash against the possibility of his call for "good schools," referred to his critics as "nitwits" (see page 200).

If this is true, and if we recognize the present attitude of white America toward black America, then the Negro not only needs the vast majority of these schools, but it is a grave question if, in the near future, he will not need more such schools, both to take care of his natural increase, and to defend him against the growing animosity of the whites. It is of course, fashionable and popular to deny this; to try to deceive ourselves into thinking that race prejudice in the United States across the Color Line is gradually softening and that slowly but surely we are coming to the time when racial animosities and class lines will be so obliterated that separate schools will be anachronisms.

Certainly, I shall welcome such a time. Just as long as Negroes are taught in Negro schools and whites in white schools; the poor in the slums, and the rich in private schools; just as long as it is impracticable to welcome Negro students to Harvard, Yale and Princeton; just as long as colleges like Williams, Amherst and Wellesley tend to become the property of certain wealthy families, where Jews are not solicited; just so long we shall lack in America that sort of public education which will create the intelligent basis of a real democracy.

Much as I would like this, and hard as I have striven and shall strive to help realize it, I am no fool; and I know that race prejudice in the United States today is such that most Negroes cannot receive proper education in white institutions. If the public schools of Atlanta, Nashville, New Orleans and Jacksonville were thrown open to all races tomorrow, the education that colored children would get in them would be worse than pitiable. It would not be education. And in the same way, there are many public school systems in the North where Negroes are admitted and tolerated, but they are not educated; they are crucified. There are certain Northern universities where Negro students, no matter what their ability, desert, or accomplishment, cannot get fair recognition, either in classroom or on the campus, in dining halls and student activities, or in common human courtesy. It is well-known that in certain faculties of the University of Chicago, no Negro has yet received the doctorate and seldom can achieve the mastership in arts; at Harvard, Yale and Columbia, Negroes are admitted but not welcomed; while in other institutions, like Princeton, they cannot even enroll.

Under such circumstances, there is no room for argument as to whether the Negro needs separate schools or not. The plain fact faces us that either he will have separate schools or he will not be educated. There may be, and there is, considerable difference of opinion as to how far this separation in schools is today necessary. There can be argument as to what our attitude toward further separation should be. Suppose, for instance, that in Montclair, New Jersey, a city of wealth and culture, the Board of Education is determined to establish separate schools for Negroes; suppose that, despite the law, separate Negro schools are already established in Philadelphia, and pressure is being steadily brought to extend this separation at least to the junior high school; what must be our attitude toward this?

Manifestly, no general and inflexible rule can be laid down. If public opinion is such in Montclair that Negro children cannot receive decent and sympathetic education in the white schools, and no Negro teachers can be employed, there is for us no choice. We have got to accept Negro schools. Any agitation and action aimed at compelling a rich and powerful majority of the citizens to do what they will not do, is useless. On the other hand, we have a right and a duty to assure ourselves of the truth concerning this attitude; by careful conferences, by public meetings and by petitions, we should convince ourselves whether this demand for separate schools is merely the agitation of a prejudiced minority, or the considered and final judgment of the town.

There are undoubtedly cases where a minority of leaders force their opinions upon a majority, and induce a community to establish separate schools, when as a matter of fact, there is no general demand for it; there has been no friction in the schools; and Negro children have been decently treated. In that case, a firm and intelligent appeal to public opinion would eventually settle the matter. But the futile attempt to compel even by law, a group to do what it is determined not to do is a silly waste of money, time, and temper.

On the other hand, there are also cases where there has been no separation in schools and no movement toward it. And yet the treatment of Negro children in the schools, the kind of teaching and the kind of advice they get, is such that they ought to demand either a thorough-going revolution in the official attitude toward Negro students, or absolute separation in educational facilities. To endure bad schools and wrong education because the schools are "mixed" is a costly if not fatal mistake. I have long been convinced, for instance, that the Negroes in the public schools of Harlem are not getting an education that is in any sense comparable in efficiency, discipline, and human development with that which Negroes are getting in the separate public schools of Washington, D.C. And yet on its school situation, black Harlem is dumb and complacent, if not actually laudatory.

Recognizing the fact that for the vast majority of colored students in elementary, secondary, and collegiate education, there must be today separate educational institutions because of an attitude on the part of the white people which is not going materially to change in our time, our customary attitude toward these separate schools must be absolutely and definitely changed. As it is today, American Negroes almost universally disparage their own schools. They look down upon them; they often treat the Negro teachers in them with contempt; they refuse to work for their adequate support; and they refuse to join public movements to increase their efficiency.

The reason for this is quite clear, and may be divided into two parts: (1) the fear that any movement which implies segregation even as a temporary, much less as a relatively permanent institution, in the United States, is a fatal surrender of principle, which in the end will rebound and bring more evils on the Negro than he suffers today. (2) The other reason is at bottom an utter lack of faith on the part of Negroes that their race can do anything really well. If Negroes could conceive that Negroes could establish schools quite as good as or even superior to white schools; if Negro colleges were of equal grade in accomplishment and in scientific work with white colleges; then separation would be a passing incident and not a permanent evil; but as long as American Negroes believe that their race is constitutionally and permanently inferior to white people, they necessarily disbelieve in every possible Negro Institution.

The first argument is more or less metaphysical and cannot be decided *a priori* for every case. There are times when one must stand up for principle at the cost of discomfort, harm, and death. But in the case of the education of the young, you must consider not simply yourself but the children and the relation of children to life. It is difficult to think of anything more important for the development of a people than proper training for their children; and yet I have repeatedly seen wise and loving colored parents take infinite pains to force their little children into schools where the white children, white teachers, and white parents despised and resented the dark child, made mock of it, neglected or bullied it, and literally rendered its life a living hell. Such parents want their child to "fight" this thing out,—but, dear God, at and the child's whole life turned into an effort to win cheap applause at the expense of healthy individuality. In other cases, the result of the experiment may be complete ruin of character, gift; and ability and ingrained hatred of schools and men. For the kind of battle thus indicated, most children are under no circumstances suited. It is the refinement of cruelty to require it of them. Therefore, in evaluating the advantage and disadvantage of accepting race hatred as a brutal but real fact or of using a little child as a battering ram upon which its nastiness can be thrust, we must give greater value and greater emphasis to the rights of the child's own soul. We shall get a finer, better balance of spirit; an infinitely more capable and rounded personality by putting children in schools where they are wanted, and where they are happy and inspired, than in thrusting them into hells where they are ridiculed and hated.

Beyond this, lies the deeper, broader fact. If the American Negro really believed in himself; if he believed that Negro teachers can educate children according to the best standards of modern training; if he believed that Negro colleges transmit and add to science, as well as or better than other colleges, then he would bend his energies, not to escaping inescapable association with his own group, but to seeing that his group had every opportunity for its best and highest development. He would insist that his teachers be decently paid; that his in the efficiency of these institutions of learning, than in forcing himself into other institutions where he is not wanted.

As long as the Negro student wishes to graduate from Columbia, not because Columbia is an institution of learning, but because it is attended by white students; as long as a Negro student is ashamed to attend Fisk or Howard because these institutions are largely run by black folk, just so long the main problem of Negro education will not be segregation but self-knowledge and self-respect.

There are not many teachers in Negro schools who would not esteem it an unparalleled honor and boast of it to their dying day, if instead of teaching black folk, they could get a chance to teach poor-whites, Irishmen, Italians or Chinese in a "white" institution. This is not unnatural. This is to them a sort of acid test of their worth. It is but the logical result of the "white" propaganda which has swept civilization for the last thousand years, and which is now bolstered and defended by brave words, high wages, and monopoly of opportunities. But this state of mind is suicidal and must be fought, and fought doggedly and bitterly: first, by giving Negro teachers decent wages, decent schoolhouses and equipment, and reasonable chances for advancement; and then by kicking out and leaving to the mercy of the white world those who, do not and cannot believe in their own.

Lack of faith in Negro enterprise upon them by dominant white public opinion, they will suddenly lose interest and scarcely raise a finger to see, that the resultant, Negro schools get a fair share of the public funds so as to have adequate equipment and housing; to see that real teachers are appointed, and that they are paid as much as white teachers doing the same work. Today, when the Negro public school system gets from half to one-tenth of the amount of money spent on white schools, and is often consequently poorly run and poorly taught, colored people tacitly if not openly join with white people in assuming that Negroes cannot run Negro enterprises, and cannot educate themselves, and that the very establishment of a Negro school means starting an inferior school.

The N.A.A.C.P. and other Negro organizations have spent thousands of dollars to prevent the establishment of segregated Negro schools, but scarcely a single cent to see that the division of funds between white and Negro schools, North and South, is carried out with some faint approximation of justice. There can be no doubt that if the Supreme Court were overwhelmed with cases where the blatant and impudent discrimination against Negro education is openly acknowledged, it would be compelled to hand down decisions which would make this discrimination impossible. We Negroes do not dare to press this point and force these decisions because, forsooth, it would acknowledge the fact of separate schools, a fact that does not need to be acknowledged, and will not need to be for two centuries.

Howard, Fisk, and Atlanta are naturally unable to do the type and grade of graduate work which is done at Columbia, Chicago, and Harvard; but why attribute this to a defect in the Negro race, and not to the fact that the large white colleges have from one hundred to one thousand times the funds for equipment and research that Negro colleges can command? To this, it may logically be answered, all the more reason that Negroes should try to get into better-equipped schools, and who pray denies this? But the opportunity for such entrance is becoming more and more difficult, and the training offered less and less suited to the American Negro of today. Conceive a Negro teaching in a Southern school the economics which he learned at the Harvard Business School! Conceive a Negro teacher of history retailing to his black students the sort of history that is taught at the University of Chicago! Imagine the history of Reconstruction being handed by a colored professor from the lips of Columbia professors to the ears of the black belt! The results of this kind of thing are often fantastic, and call for Negro history and sociology, and even physical science taught by men who understand their audience, and are not afraid of the truth.

There was a time when the ability of Negro brains to do first-class work had to be proven by facts and figures, and I was a part of the movement that sought to set the accomplishments of Negro ability before the world. But the world before which I was setting this proof was a disbelieving white world. I did not need the proof for myself. I did not dream that my fellow Negroes needed it; but in the last few years, I have become curiously convinced that until American Negroes believe in their own power and ability, they are going to be helpless before the white world, and the white world, realizing this inner paralysis and lack of self-confidence, is going to persist in its insane determination to rule the universe for its own selfish advantage.

Does the Negro need separate schools? God knows he does. But what he needs more than separate schools is a firm and unshakable belief that twelve million American Negroes have the inborn capacity to accomplish just as much as any nation of twelve million anywhere in the world ever accomplished, and that this is not because they are Negroes but because they are human.

So far, I have noted chiefly negative arguments for separate Negro institutions of learning based on the fact that in the majority of cases Negroes are not welcomed in public schools and universities nor treated as fellow human beings. But beyond this, there are certain positive reasons due to the fact that American Negroes have, because of their history, group experiences and memories, a distinct entity, whose spirit and reactions demand a certain type of education for its development.

In the past, this fact has been noted and misused for selfish purposes. On the ground that Negroes needed type of education "suited" to them, we have an attempt to train them as menials and dependents; or in the case of West Indians, an attempt to perpetuate their use as low-paid laborers by limiting their knowledge; or in the case of African natives, efforts to deprive them of modern languages and modern science in order to seal their subordination to out-worn mores, reactionary native rulers, industrialization.

What I have in mind is nothing like this. It is rather an honest development of the premises from which this plea for special education starts. It is illustrated by these facts: Negroes must know the history of the Negro race in America, and this they will seldom get in white institutions. Their children ought to study textbooks like Brawley's "Short History," the first edition of Woodson's "Negro in Our History," and Cromwell, Turner and

Dykes' "Readings from Negro Authors." Negroes who celebrate the birthdays of Washington and Lincoln, and the worthy, but colorless and relatively unimportant "founders" of various Negro colleges, ought not to forget the 5th of March,—that first national holiday of this country, which commemorates the martyrdom of Crispus Attucks. They ought to celebrate Negro Health Week and Negro History Week. They ought to study intelligently and from their own point of view, the slave trade, slavery, emancipation, Reconstruction, and present economic development.

Beyond this, Negro colleges ought to be studying anthropology, psychology, and the social sciences, from the point of view of the colored races. Today, the anthropology that is being taught, and the expeditions financed for archeological and ethnographical explorations, are for the most part straining every nerve to erase the history of black folk from the record. One has only to remember that the majority of anthropologists have peopled the continent of Africa itself with almost no Negroes, while men like Sayee and Reisner have even declared that the Ethiopians have no Negro blood! All this has been done by the legerdemain and metaphysics of nomenclature, and in the face of the great and important history of black blood in the world.

Recently, something has been done by colored scholars to correct the extraordinary propaganda of post-war psychology which sent men like Brigham and McDougall rushing into scientific proof of Negro congenital inferiority. But much more is necessary and demanded of Negro scholarship. In history and the social sciences the Negro school and college has an unusual opportunity and role. It does not consist simply in trying to parallel the history of white folk with similar boasting about black and brown folk, but rather an honest evaluation of human effort and accomplishment, without color blindness, and without transforming history into a record of dynasties and prodigies.

Here, we have in America, a working class which in our day has achieved physical freedom, and mental clarity. An economic battle has just begun. It can be studied and guided; it can teach consumers' cooperation, democracy, and socialism, and be made not simply a record and pattern for the Negro race, but a guide for the rise of the working classes throughout the world, just at the critical time when these classes are about to assume their just political domination which is destined to become the redemption of mankind.

Much has been said of the special esthetic ability of the Negro race. Naturally, it has been exaggerated. Naturally, it is not a racial characteristic in the sense of hereditary, inborn, and heritable difference; but there is no doubt but what the tremendous psychic history of the American and West Indian groups has made it possible for the present generation to accumulate a wealth of material which, with encouragement and training, could find expression in the drama, in color and form, and in music. And no where could this training better be pursued than in separate Negro schools under competent and intelligent teachers? What little has already been done in this line is scarcely a beginning of what is possible, provided the object is not simple entertainment or bizarre efforts at money raising.

In biology, the pioneering work of Carolyn Bond Day could be extended indefinitely in Negro laboratories; and in the purely physical and chemical sciences, the need of Negroes familiar with the intricate technical basis of modern civilization would not only help them to find their place in the industrial scene for their own organization, but also enable them to help Abyssinia, India, China, and the colored world, to maintain their racial integrity, and their economic independence. It could easily be the mission and duty of American Negroes to master this scientific basis of modern invention, and give it to all mankind.

Thus, instead of our schools being simply separate schools, forced on us by grim necessity, they can become centers of a new and beautiful effort at human education, which may easily lead and guide the world in many important and valuable aspects. It is for this reason that when our schools are separate, the control of the teaching force, the expenditure of money, the choice of textbooks, the discipline and other administrative matters of this sort ought, also, to come into our hands, and be incessantly demanded and guarded.

I remember once, in Texas, reading in a high-school textbook for colored students, the one anecdote given concerning Abraham Lincoln: he was pictured as chasing Negro thieves all night through the woods from his Mississippi flatboat! Children could read that history in vain to learn any word of what had been accomplished ill American history by Benjamin Banneker, Jan Matseliger, Elijah McCoy, Frederick Douglass, or James Dunn. In fact, one of the peculiar tragedies of the smaller Southern colleges is that they hire as teachers of history, economics and sociology, colored men trained in Northern institutions where not a word of any information concerning these disciplines, so far as Negroes are concerned, has ever been imparted to them. I speak from experience, because I came to Atlanta University to teach history in 1897, without the slightest idea from my Harvard tuition, that Negroes ever had any history!

I know that this article will forthwith be interpreted by certain illiterate "nitwits" as a plea for segregated Negro schools and colleges. It is not. It is simply calling a spade a spade. It is saying in plain English: that a separate Negro school, where children are treated like human beings, trained by teachers of their own race, who know what it means to be black in the year of salvation 1935, is infinitely better than making our boys and girls doormats to be spit and trampled upon and lied to by ignorant social climbers, whose sole claim to superiority is ability to kick "niggers" when they are down. I say, too, that certain studies and discipline necessary to Negroes can seldom be found in white schools.

It means this, and nothing more.

To sum up this: theoretically, the Negro needs neither segregated schools nor mixed schools. What he needs is Education. What he must remember is that there is no magic, either in mixed schools or in segregated schools. A mixed school with poor and unsympathetic teachers, with hostile public opinion, and no teaching of truth concerning black folk, is bad. A segregated school with ignorant placeholders, inadequate equipment; poor salaries, and wretched housing, is equally bad. Other things being equal, the mixed school is the broader, more natural basis for the education of all youth. It gives wider contacts; it inspires greater self-confidence; and suppresses the inferiority, complex. But other things seldom are equal, and in that case, Sympathy, Knowledge, and the Truth, outweigh all that the mixed school can offer.

The Talented Tenth: Re-examination of a Concept (1948)[33]

Some years ago I used the phrase "The Talented Tenth," meaning leadership of the Negro race in America by a trained few. Since then this idea has been criticized. It has been said that I had in mind the building of an aristocracy with neglect of the masses. This criticism has seemed even more valid because of emphasis on the meaning and power of the mass of people to which Karl Marx gave voice in the middle of the nineteenth century, and which has been growing in influence ever since. There have come other changes in these days, which a great many of us do to realize as Revolution through which we are passing. Because of this, it is necessary to examine the world about us and our thoughts and attitudes toward it. I want then to re-examine and restate the thesis of the Talented Tenth which I laid down many years ago.

In a day when culture is comparatively static, a man once grounded in the fundamentals of knowledge, received through current education, can depend on the more or less routine absorption of knowledge for keeping up with the world. This was true for decades during the nineteenth century, and usually has been true in the slow drift of many other centuries. But today, the tide runs swiftly, and almost every fundamental concept which most of us learned in college has undergone radical change; so that a man who was broadly educated in 1900 may be widely ignorant in 1948, unless he has made conscious, continuous, and determined

---

33   Originally appeared in *The Boule Journal* October, 1948. Often referred to as "Talented Tenth Memorial Address," this speech was delivered to the Sigma Phi Pi Fraternity, August 13, 1948 on the campus of Wilberforce University, in Xenia, Ohio.

"The Talented Tenth Memorial Address," *The Boulé Journal*, v.15, n.1 (October 1948). Reprinted by permission of Sigma Pi Phi Fraternity.

effort to keep abreast with the development of knowledge and of thought in the last half century. For instance, since 1900 physics and chemistry have been revolutionized in many of their basic concepts. Astronomy is today almost a new science as compared with the time of Copernicus. Psychology has risen from guess-work and introspection to an exact science. Biology and Anthropology have changed and expanded widely; History and Sociology have begun in the middle of the twentieth century, first, to take on the shape of real sciences rather than being largely theory and opinion.

If, now, a college man of 1900, or even of 1925, has spent his time since graduation mainly in making a living, he is in fair way not to be able to understand the world of 1950. It is necessary then for men of education continually to readjust their knowledge, and this is doubly necessary in this day of swift revolution in ideas, in ideals, in industrial techniques, in rapid travel, and in varieties and kinds of human contacts.

Turn now to that complex of social problems, which surrounds and conditions our life, and which we call more or less vaguely, The Negro Problem. It is clear that in 1900, American Negroes were an inferior caste, were frequently lynched and mobbed, widely disfranchised, and usually segregated in the main areas of life. As student and worker at that time, I looked upon them and saw salvation through intelligent leadership; as I said, through a "Talented Tenth." And for this intelligence, I argued, we needed college-trained men. Therefore, I stressed college and higher training.

Video Sidebar

Westbrook talks about W.E.B. Du Bois' speech that marks the beginning of his downfall, where he compares his expectations for "The Talented Tenth" with disappointing outcomes.

http://youtu.be/gXZghG2Q7oY

For these men with their college training there would be needed thorough understanding of the mass of Negroes and their problems; and, therefore, I emphasized scientific study. Willingness to work and make personal sacrifice for solving these problems was of course, the first prerequisite and *sine qua non*. I did not stress this, I assumed it.

There was no lack of small and selfish souls; there were among the student body careless and lazy fellows; and there were especially sharp young persons, who received the education given very cheaply at Fisk University, with the distinct and single-minded idea, of seeing how much they could make out of it for themselves, and nobody else.

When I came out of college into the world of work, I realized that it was quite possible that my plan of training a talented tenth might put in control and power, a group of selfish, self-indulgent, well-to-do men, whose basic interest in solving the Negro problem was personal; personal freedom and unhampered enjoyment and use of the world, without any real care, or certainly no arousing care, as to what became of the mass of American Negroes, or of the mass of any people. My Talented Tenth, I could see, might result in a sort of interracial free-for-all, with the devil taking the hindmost and the foremost taking anything they could lay hands on. This, historically, has always been the danger of aristocracy. It was for a long time regarded as, almost inevitable because of the scarcity of ability among men and because, naturally the aristocrat came to regard himself and his whims as necessarily the end and only end of civilization and culture. As long as the masses supported this doctrine, aristocracy and mass misery lived amiably together.

Into this situation came the revolutionary thought, first voiced in former ages by great moral leaders, which asked charity for the poor and sympathy for the ignorant and sick. And even intimated eventual justice in Heaven. But in the suddenly expanding economy and marvelous technique of the eighteenth and nineteenth centuries, there came prophets and reformers, but especially the voice of Karl Marx, to say that the poor need not always be with us, and that all men could and should be free from poverty.

Karl Marx stressed the fact that not merely the upper class but the mass of men were the real people of the world. He insisted that the masses were poor, ignorant, and sick, not by sin or by nature but by oppression. He preached that planned production of goods and just distribution of income would abolish poverty, ignorance and disease, and make the so-called upper-class, not the exception, but the rule among mankind. He declared that the world was not for the few, but for the many; that out of the masses of men could come overwhelming floods of ability and genius, if we freed men by plan and not by rare chance. Civilization not only could be shared by the vast majority of men, but such civilization founded on a wide human base would be better and more enduring than anything that the world has seen. The world would thus escape the enduring danger of being run by a selfish few for their own advantage.

Very gradually as the philosophy of Karl Marx and many of his successors seeped into my understanding, I tried to apply this doctrine with regard to Negroes. My Talented Tenth must be more than talented, and work not simply as individuals. Its passport to leadership was not alone learning but expert knowledge of modern economics as it affected American Negroes; and in addition to this and fundamental, would be its willingness to sacrifice and plan for such economic revolution in industry and just distribution of wealth, as would make the rise of our group possible...

In this reorientation of my ideas, my pointing out the new knowledge necessary for leadership, and new ideas of race and culture, there still remains that fundamental and basic requirement of character for any successful leadership toward great ideals.

Even if the ideals are clearly perceived, honesty of character and purity of motive are needed without which no effort succeeds or deserves to succeed. We used to talk much of character—perhaps too much. At Fisk, we had it dinned into our ears. At Harvard we never mentioned it. We thought of it: but it was not good taste to talk of it: At Berlin we quite forgot it. But that was reaction. We cannot have perfection. We have few saints. But we must have honest men or we die. We must have unselfish, far-seeing leadership or we fail.

What can Sigma Pi Phi do to see that we get it for the American Negro? So far as the group before me is concerned little can be done, for the simple reason that most of our present membership will soon be dead. Unless we begin to recruit this fraternity membership with young men and large numbers of them, our biennial conclaves will be increasingly devoted to obituaries. We should have a large increase of membership, drawn from men who have received their college education since the First World War. This new membership must not simply be successful in the American sense of being rich; they must not all be physicians and lawyers. The technicians, business men, teachers and social workers admitted must be those who realize the economic revolution now sweeping the world, and do not think that private profit is the measure of public welfare. And too: we must deliberately seek honest men.

This screened young membership must be far greater in number than it is now. Baltimore for instance has more than 166,000 Negroes and only 23 in its Boule, representing less than 100 persons. Surely there must be at least 23 other persons in Baltimore worthy of fellowship. It is inconceivable that we should even for a moment dream that with a membership of 440 we have scratched even the tip of the top of the surface of a group representative of potential Negro leadership in America. Nothing but congenital laziness should keep us from a membership of 3,000 by the next biennium without any lowering of quality; and a membership of 30,000 by 1960. This would be an actual numerical one hundredth of our race: a body large enough really to represent all. Yet small enough to insure exceptional quality; if screened for intelligent and disinterested planning.

Having gotten a group of predominantly active virile men of middle age and settled opinions, who have finished their education and begun their life work, what can they do? They must first of all recognize the fact that their own place in life is primarily a matter of opportunity, rather than simple desert or ability. That if such opportunity were extended and broadened, a thousand times as many Negroes could join the ranks of the educated, and able, instead of sinking into poverty, disease and crime; that the primary duty of this organization would be to find desert, ability, and character among young Negroes and get for them education and opportunity; that the major opportunity should be seen as work according to gift and training with pay sufficient to furnish a decent standard of living.

A national organization of this sort must be prepared to use propaganda, make investigation, plan procedures and even finance projects. This will call for an initial body of belief which even now can be forecast in outline.

We would want to impress on the emerging generations of Negroes in America, the ideal of plain living and high thinking, in defiance of American noise, waste and display; the rehabilitation of the indispensable family group, by deliberate planning of marriages, with mates selected for heredity, physique, health and brains, with less insistence on color, comeliness or romantic sex lure, miscalled love; youth should marry young and have a limited number of healthy children; the home must be a place of education, rather than cleaning and cooking, with books, discussion and entertainment.

The schools where these children are sent must not be chosen for the color of their teachers or students, but for their efficiency in educating a particular child. In home and out children should learn not to neglect our art heritage: music is not designed solely for night clubs; drama is not aimed at Broadway; dancing is not the handmaid of prostitution; and writing is not mainly for income.

Our religion with all of its dogma, demagoguery and showmanship, can be a center to teach character, right conduct and sacrifice. There lies here a career for a Negro Gandhi and a host of earnest followers.

The dark hosts of Liberia and Ethiopia and other parts of Africa together with Asia, the Pacific lands, South and Central America, and the Caribbean area, have need for that broad knowledge of the world and special training in technique which we might learn and take to them.

They do not need us for exploitation and get-rich-quick schemes. There is no reason why the sort of thought and teaching which two thousand years ago made the groves of Athens the center of the world's salvation, could not live again in ten thousand Negro homes in America today.

Occupation should not, and need not, be left to chance or confined to what whites are doing, or are willing to let us do. It must involve innovation and experiment. It must be a carefully planned; thoroughly thought-out with wide study of human wants, technical power, trained effort and consecrated devotion with the use of every scientific procedure in physics, chemistry, biology, psychology, sociology and history.

For this central object of planned work, this organization should assemble the best knowledge and experience. It should encourage pioneering and adventure; attacking desert places with modern technique; producing new goods by new processes; avoiding the factory system and mass production as the last word in work, and returning to the ideal of personal consumption, personal taste and human desire; thinking of consumption and the consumers as coming before production, and not of production as the end of industry and profit as its motive.

The new generation must learn that the object of the world is not profit but service and happiness. They must therefore be directed away from careers which are anti-social and dishonest, but immensely profitable. Insurance can be a social help but much of it today is organized theft. We must have drug stores, but the patent nostrums in which so many of them deal deserve the penitentiary. Gambling not only as poker-playing but as a profitable career, is seeping through all kinds of American business from the stock market, factory and wholesale store, to the numbers racket, horse racing, and radio gifts, Every effort should be made to warn the next generation away from this dry rot of death and crimes.

An organization adapted to such a program of propaganda and work of guidance, and able to search for and select ability and character and finance efforts to give it opportunity, will need large funds at its disposal. The sacrifice necessary to provide such funds should be regarded not as sentimental charity or mushy religious fervor but as foresight and investment in the future of the Negro in America, and canny insurance against loss by wholesale neglect of invaluable human resources. We may reach the high ideal when again the tithe, the tenth of our income will go to the perfectly feasible effort of so civilizing the American Negro that he will be able to lead the world and will want to do so.

This, then is my re-examined and restated theory of the "Talented Tenth," which has thus become the doctrine of the "Guiding Hundredth."

Naturally, I do not dream, that a word of mine will transform, to any essential degree, the form and trends of this fraternity; but I am certain the idea called for expression and that the seed must be dropped whether in this or other soil, today or tomorrow.

Video Sidebar

"The Talented Tenth Memorial Address" marks the end of his public speaking career because he started a scorched earth policy, berating Blacks for not working harder to better themselves.

http://youtu.be/zELXwADc448

W.E.B. Du Bois Selected Bibliography

Throughout his life, W.E.B. Du Bois wrote hundreds of articles, speeches, essays and book chapters, as well as poetry, songs, plays and other informative and creative works. Below is a select list of books written by W.E.B. Du Bois.

Du Bois, W.E.B. *The Suppression of the African Slave Trade to the United States of America, 1638-1870*. New York: Longmans, Green and Co., 1896.

―――. *The Philadelphia Negro: A Social Study*. Philadelphia: University of Philadelphia, 1899.

―――. *The Souls of Black Folk*. Chicago: A.C. McClurg & Co., 1903.

―――. *John Brown*. Philadelphia: G.W. Jacobs & Company, 1909.

―――. *Quest of the Silver Fleece*. Chicago: A.C. McClurg & Co., 1911.

―――. *Darkwater: Voices from Within the Veil*. New York: Harcourt, Brace and Howe, 1920.

―――. *The Gift of Black Folk: The Negro in the Making of America*. Boston: The Stratford Co., 1924.

―――. *Black Reconstruction: An Essay Toward a History of the Part Which Black Folk Played in the Attempt to Reconstruct Democracy in America, 1860-1880*. New York: Harcourt, Brace and Co., 1935.

―――. *Black Folk, Then And Now: An Essay in the History and Sociology of the Negro Race*. New York: H. Holt and Company, 1939.

―――. *Dusk of Dawn: An Essay Toward an Autobiography of a Race Concept*. New York: Harcourt, Brace and Company, 1940.

―――. *The World And Africa: An Inquiry into the Part Which Africa has Played in World History*. New York: The Viking Press, 1947.

―――. *In Battle For Peace: The Story of My 83rd Birthday*. New York: Masses & Mainstream, 1952.

―――. *The Ordeal of Mansart*. New York: Mainstream Publishers, 1957.

―――. *Mansart Builds a School*. New York: Mainstream Publishers, 1959.

―――. *Worlds of Color*. New York : Mainstream Publishers, 1961.

―――. *The Autobiography of W.E.B. Du Bois: A Soliloquy on Viewing My Life From the Last Decade of Its First Century*. New York: International Publishers, 1968.

ADDITIONAL VIDEOS

Du Bois' 80-year writing career is what made him remarkable.

http://youtu.be/OAZgOjLNIE0

W.E.B. Du Bois' educational thought is overshadowed by his career in politics and civil rights.

http://youtu.be/ronnumIZ6u8

Du Bois will always be relevant where there are people who are disenfranchised.

http://youtu.be/2osh3RWxa5o

You were either in favor or not in favor of Du Bois depending on whether or not you agreed with his beliefs.

http://youtu.be/R-5o4IF5QnM

Du Bois' strong political career overshadowed his philosophy on education, which is why his writings are not examined closely enough.

http://youtu.be/KB285CAUrBo

Nearly all of Du Bois' ideas are implemented, but Westbrook would like the concept of gender or culturally specific schools to be re-visited.

http://youtu.be/R_J6JT2ONIw

Are W.E.B. DuBois' educational ideas applicable to other cultures in the United States and throughout the world?

http://youtu.be/7XJGFSPIosA

Westbrook describes being present when David Levering Lewis received the call that he won the Pulitzer Prize for his W.E.B. Du Bois biography.

http://youtu.be/JrhfO1xrUzo

ABOUT THE EDITOR

RANDALL WESTBROOK is a faculty member at the School of Education at Fairleigh Dickinson University, Madison, New Jersey. He has taught courses in Education and in Africana Studies at Rutgers University. His scholarly work focuses on the life and educational thought of W.E.B. Du Bois (1868–1963), specializing in work from 1883–1903. Westbrook has contributed to publications such as the *Harvard Journal for Racial and Ethnic Justice*, *The Lincoln Journal for Social and Political Thought*, and the *Journal for African American History*. Additionally, he has contributed to the textbook *The Black Experience in America* (2011).

Westbrook earned his master's and doctoral degrees from Rutgers University. His doctoral study on Du Bois focused on Du Bois' contributions to educational thought prior to 1905.

Westbrook's expertise on the young Du Bois has garnered him appearances as a featured lecturer at birthday anniversary celebrations in Du Bois' birthplace of Great Barrington, Massachusetts in 2007 and 2008.

Video Sidebar

Randall Westbrook describes his journey as a W.E.B. Du Bois scholar and what inspired him to fill in the gaps of analysis of Du Bois' educational thought.
http://youtu.be/7sgROyRd4JA

CPSIA information can be obtained
at www.ICGtesting.com
Printed in the USA
BVHW040252260821
615090BV00010B/151